100 Ideas for
Secondary Teachers:

Engaging Parents

Other titles in the 100 Ideas for Secondary Teachers series:

100 Ideas for Secondary Teachers: Outstanding Lessons
by Ross Morrison McGill

100 Ideas for Secondary Teachers: Managing Behaviour
by Johnnie Young

100 Ideas for Secondary Teachers: Outstanding Mathematics Lessons
by Mike Ollerton

100 Ideas for Secondary Teachers: Outstanding English Lessons
by Angella Cooze and Mary Myatt

100 Ideas for Secondary Teachers: Assessment for Learning
by David Spendlove

100 Ideas for Secondary Teachers: Outstanding Science Lessons
by Ian McDaid

100 Ideas for Secondary Teachers: Supporting Students with Dyslexia
by Gavin Reid and Shannon Green

100 Ideas for Secondary Teachers: Revision
by John Mitchell

100 Ideas for Secondary Teachers: Outstanding Geography Lessons
by David Rogers

100 Ideas for Secondary Teachers: Outstanding History Lessons
by Emily Thomas

100 Ideas for Secondary Teachers: Engaging Learners
by Jon Tait

100 Ideas for Secondary Teachers: Supporting Students with Numeracy Difficulties
by Patricia Babtie and Sue Dillon

100 Ideas for Secondary Teachers: Outstanding MFL Lessons
by Dannielle Warren

100 Ideas for Secondary Teachers: Stretch and Challenge
by Paul Wright

100 Ideas for Secondary Teachers: Outstanding RE Lessons
by Andy Lewis

100 Ideas for Secondary Teachers:

Engaging Parents

Janet Goodall and Kathryn Weston

BLOOMSBURY EDUCATION

LONDON   OXFORD   NEW YORK   NEW DELHI   SYDNEY

BLOOMSBURY EDUCATION

Bloomsbury Publishing Plc

50 Bedford Square, London, WC1B 3DP, UK

BLOOMSBURY, BLOOMSBURY EDUCATION and the Diana logo are
trademarks of Bloomsbury Publishing Plc

First published in Great Britain, 2020

A catalogue record for this book is available from the British Library

ISBN: PB: 978-1-4729-7663-5; ePDF: 978-1-4729-7664-2;
ePub: 978-1-4729-7661-1

2 4 6 8 10 9 7 5 3 1 (paperback)

Typeset by Newgen KnowledgeWorks Pvt. Ltd., Chennai, India
Printed and bound in the UK by CPI Group Ltd, Croydon, CR0 4YY

All papers used by Bloomsbury Publishing Plc are natural, recyclable products
from wood grown in well managed forests. The manufacturing processes
conform to the environmental regulations of the country of origin

To find out more about our authors and books visit
www.bloomsbury.com and sign up for our newsletters

I would like to dedicate this book to Daniel and Catherine Goodall, my own children, who have grown from the teenagers they were into adults of whom I am very proud. (And yes, I do tell them!)

Dr Janet Goodall

I would like to dedicate this book to David Weston or 'Uncle Didi', the best uncle, brother-in-law, role model, teacher and supporter of teachers.

Dr Kathryn Weston

Contents

Introduction   x
How to use this book   xi

Part 1: Background   **1**
1 Parental involvement vs parental engagement 2
2 Why this book will save you time   4
3 Purposeful picking and choosing   5
4 Assets are better than deficits   6
5 From achievement gap to educational debt   7
6 Home learning environments matter –
     even for teenagers   8
7 Partnership working with parents   9
8 A wish-list for partnership   10
9 Eyes on the prize: it's all about learning   12

Part 2: A whole-school effort   **13**
10 What do we believe?   14
11 Learning across the school   16
12 Judge not...   17
13 Think beyond the classroom   18
14 The importance of school leadership   19
15 Ditch the school improvement plan   20
16 Support support staff   22
17 The perils of policy (borrowing)   24
18 Change the discourse   25
19 Model learning and let parents know   26
20 Beware the power-play   28
21 PTA, parent council, parent forum...
     use your groups   29
22 Old skills, new uses   30

Part 3: What's special about secondary?   **31**
23 What's different about this phase?   32
24 What does 'parent' mean for
     secondary students?   33
25 All parents, not just the usual few   34
26 The importance of parental self-efficacy   36
27 The importance of parent-to-parent work   37

28 Working together across subjects   38
29 Working with feeder schools   39
30 It's not a matter of money   40
31 Reporting back to parents   41
32 Reporting to support   42

**Part 4: Understanding the parents
of teenagers   45**
33 Parenting is different for teenagers –
but still vital   46
34 Transitioning transition   48
35 Working parents = tired parents   50
36 Parents of young people with
additional needs   51
37 Are teachers human?   52
38 Handbook for Year 7 families   53
39 Supporting family learning   54
40 Not every child is in a family   56
41 Parents are teenagers who grew up   57
42 Who are your parents?   58
43 Planning for parents   59
44 Watch your language   60
45 Find out what parents want   62

**Part 5: Setting up to support –
an iterative process   63**
46 ROIDH – records or it didn't happen   64
47 Did it work?   66
48 Getting governors on board   68
49 In the community or part of
the community?   69
50 Opening the school gates   70
51 What does your website say about you?   71
52 Making the most of the website   72
53 Pictures tell a thousand words   74
54 Tracking communications   75
55 Policies in plain (language)   76
56 Keeping track of it all in a large school   77
57 Get out of school   78
58 Social media and phones in school   79

**Part 6: Vault (or at least surmount)
the barriers   81**
59 (Re)building bridges   82
60 Beware when talking barriers   83
61 Language barriers: part one   84
62 Careful of the cost   86

63 World Book Day	88
64 Language barriers: part two	90
65 Summer needn't mean no learning	91
66 Giving information vs dialogue	92
67 You said, we did	94
68 Having difficult conversations	95

Part 7: Helping parents to help **97**

69 How was your day?	98
70 Worry not	99
71 Share red flags early on	100
72 Supporting resilience	101
73 What do parents want to know? What do they need to know?	102
74 Sleep matters	103
75 Don't wait to support aspirations	104
76 'University's too expensive for us!'	106
77 Don't neglect the usual suspects	107
78 Not all bad all the time	108
79 Managing maths and learned helplessness in families	110
80 Supporting parents of the digital generation	111
81 Setting the course for coursework	112
82 Study skills – mind the gap!	113
83 It's OK not to know the answer (helping parents towards mastery)	114
84 Parents and homework	115
85 Use effective praise with teenagers (and their parents!)	116
86 Who does what? (Teacher vs parent roles)	117
87 The parents you never see	118
88 Reflect then innovate	119
89 Keep talking	120
90 'Proud of you' letters	121
91 Parent peer support	122

Part 8: Sustainable practice **123**

92 It's everyone's job	124
93 Have a party!	125
94 Not my circus, not my monkeys	126
95 Every failure is an opportunity	127
96 Don't start from scratch	128
97 Being a reflective practitioner	129
98 Utilise the expertise already around	130
99 Using the skills you have	131
100 Not quite finis...	132

Introduction

Although research has shown that parental engagement tends to drop off as children age, research has *also* shown that parents' engagement with their children's learning remains important throughout the secondary years. The form that engagement takes changes as children age, as one would expect – after all, parents' relationships and dealings with their children are very different in secondary school than they were when the children were toddlers. As children go through adolescence, they attain more independence, and often come to rely more on their peers. But parents remain an important mainstay for many young people; in our research, secondary students have told us quite clearly that what is important to them is that someone shows an interest in what they are doing and learning.

We wrote this book at the request of teachers and staff in secondary schools; they'd seen *100 Ideas for Primary Teachers: Engaging Parents* and wanted a book that was targeted for their setting, to support their work with parents. There are some ideas here that are parallel to the ideas in our first book; that's not terribly surprising because young people are still young people and parents are still parents (and teachers are still teachers!). But there are differences between primary and secondary schools (as well as middle schools) and we've tried to reflect and support those differences in this book.

We're fairly sure no one has ever said that raising or teaching teenagers is easy, and we're not going to pretend it is. We are, however, hoping that the ideas in this book will help you, as members of school staff, to engage with the parents and families of young people to support learning.

One final point to note before we get started: it's important to realise at the very outset that when we say 'parents', we mean 'adults with a significant caring responsibility for the young person' – so it could be a parent, a grandparent or other family member, a foster parent, a friend... it's a wide-ranging term.

How to use this book

This book includes quick, easy and practical ideas for you to dip in and out of to help you to engage parents in students' learning.

Each idea includes:

- a catchy title, easy to refer to and share with your colleagues
- an interesting quote linked to the idea
- a summary of the idea in bold, making it easy to flick through the book and identify an idea you want to use at a glance
- information about the idea or a step-by-step guide to implementing it.

Each idea also includes one or more of the following:

Teaching tip

Practical tips and advice for how and how not to run the activity or put the idea into practice.

Taking it further

Ideas and advice for how to extend the idea or develop it further.

Bonus idea ★

There are 43 bonus ideas in this book that are extra-exciting, extra-original and extra-interesting.

Share how you use these ideas and find out what other practitioners have done using **#100ideas**.

Online resources also accompany this book. When a resource is referenced in the book, follow the link **www.bloomsbury.com/100-ideas-secondary-engaging-parents** to find extra resources, catalogued under the relevant idea number.

Background

Part 1

Parental involvement vs parental engagement

'Our parental engagement is fine – we get over 80 per cent turnout to parents' evening every year. I really wish parents would leave us to it. These children are all grown up now.'

There's a difference between parental involvement with schools and parental engagement with learning. Most of the tips in this book are aimed at increasing parental engagement with learning – not at getting parents into school.

Parental *involvement* with school and schooling can take the form of:

- attending parents' evenings, tutor days or other achievement- or reporting-focused meetings
- coming into school for concerts, assemblies, plays, sports days or cake sales
- accompanying teaching staff on school trips
- discussing school matters with teaching staff.

These aren't bad things to do, but they are bad places to stop. They are just a first step, and are much easier for some parents than for others.

Parental *engagement* with learning, however, includes anything where family members interact with young people to support their learning:

- discussions about learning, current events, politics, social issues, social media and favourite films, between family members and young people
- asking how the young person's day at school went; even though this question rarely seems to get answered, young people have told us that they take it as a sign that 'someone cares' about them

- going to museums, visiting friends and families, family outings, reading together, watching TV and films together and discussing them
- making a cup of tea for a student during homework or revision time, and ensuring that they have a quiet place to work.

Parental involvement with schooling is fine but unlikely to support the learners who are struggling in our current system, and also unlikely to support their parents. Parental engagement with learning, however, has been clearly shown by the literature to lead to increases in attendance, homework return, and academic and social outcomes. Parental engagement in learning is our interest in this book.

Taking it further

Don't assume what parents are doing with their young people; throughout this book we suggest a number of ways and times to ask parents for information. Dialogue goes both ways!

Why this book will save you time

'You want me to do something else? When do you think I will have time to do all these things?'

Teachers are overworked; most work long after the nominal school day has finished. On top of actual teaching and the usual accompanying work (planning, assessment, CPD, and so on), there are now expectations in the areas of health and wellbeing and even crime prevention.

Teaching tip

You may recognise some of the ideas in this book from our previous book about engaging parents in the primary phase. That's because while some things change as children grow up, many things don't. If you're a parent with smaller children, don't neglect your own experiences as a basis for work – and don't be afraid to share those experiences with the parents of your students!

So why are we asking teaching staff to take on yet another project: engaging parents? How will they have time and why should they take that time? The simple answer is that it benefits their students, which is, after all, the main reason for being involved in schooling. That's the touchstone, the basis for all work with families: we all want the same thing, namely the best outcomes for our young people.

We know from experience and the literature that *effective* parental engagement in young people's learning can have beneficial impacts on attendance, rates of homework return, engagement in learning, achievement and outcomes. When you consider the time that teachers spend dealing with late or non-existent homework, or attendance matters, it makes sense to investigate something that can have positive impacts in these and other areas.

Is engaging parents a simple, short-term goal? No. Is it worthwhile in the long run? Very much so. This book will demonstrate why it's important and how you, as school staff, can support parents to support young people. The ultimate goal is better outcomes for students, but along the way there should also be reductions in teacher workload and better relationships with students and their families.

Purposeful picking and choosing

'There's too much here; I can't do it all!'

We don't expect you to do everything in this book – it wouldn't be possible or useful! As with any other aspect of teaching, there are many great ideas out there but it takes time to work out what will and will not work for our students, families and schools.

It's the same for work with parents – not everything will work, not everything is appropriate and some things need to be done in sequence. It's much better to start slowly, with simple things such as positive messages home, than to expect parents to attend events *en masse* if they're not used to doing so.

This book is designed as a handy guide rather than a follow-each-step-in-sequence book. We're assuming that people using this book are active in schools and are therefore incredibly busy, so we've tried to make each idea clear and easy to understand and apply. That doesn't mean that each idea stands alone, any more than any other element of teaching does; it all fits together. The creative bit is *how* it fits together, for you, for your school and for your families. Parental engagement with learning is more of a process than a thing to be captured, measured and ticked off a list. It relates to learning, after all, which is itself a process.

We'd suggest starting by reading the introductory section to understand what we mean by 'parental engagement with learning' and why it's important. Then read the next section on the basics of making this work in a school. We'd then suggest looking at the contents and seeing what strikes you as appropriate, interesting and useful. No one knows your situation as well as you do.

Bonus idea ★

If there are a number of colleagues in your school interested in working through this book, choose an idea or section each and work through it that way. Try ideas out and come back together to discuss how you got on.

Assets are better than deficits

'I was trained about parental engagement – we had two whole hours on how to manage difficult conversations!'

Our experience tells us that, often, school staff approach work with parents from this sort of perspective – that parents and families are going to be difficult, at best, to deal with.

When it comes to supporting learning, you know that for the most part, it's better to take an asset-based approach: start from what the young person can already do and move on from there, rather than concentrating on what they cannot do or on past failures.

Working with parents is no different. As we keep reiterating: parents and young people are both, well, people! If you start from the point of view that parents are problematic, you can expect to keep finding problems. And indeed, this is the way in which many school staff have been trained to see parents; many teachers have told us that the only mention of parents in their initial teacher training was about having 'difficult conversations' with students' family members, which sets up parents as problems from the outset.

There are any number of ways in which parents and other family members can be assets to learning. And remember, this is about them being an asset to the young person's *learning*, not about them being an asset to the school – that's nice and useful (and we'll have some suggestions for this as we go through), but it's secondary to supporting learning.

From achievement gap to educational debt

'We do not merely have an achievement gap, we have an educational debt.' (Ladson-Billings, 2006)

For a number of years, researchers have been suggesting that we replace the term 'achievement gap' with 'educational debt'. The argument is that this highlights the fact that many of the issues causing young people from different backgrounds to achieve differently are not personal to those young people.

Instead, the issues are systemic, arising from a societal system that has long led to different outcomes for young people from different social, cultural and ethnic backgrounds. Research has also shown that some school initiatives to support parental engagement actually widen the gap – or increase the debt – rather than narrowing (or decreasing) it. These initiatives are, of course, created with the best will in the world. However, when initiatives are such that the only parents who feel comfortable attending them are those who need the support the least, the effect is that students who are already benefiting from the system benefit a little more, and students who are suffering do a little worse. Keep in mind the following:

- Thinking in terms of educational debt, rather than achievement gap, removes the personal element from underachievement, which can often be traced to systemic rather than personal issues.
- Think carefully about which parents and families need particular kinds of support.
- Understand that if staff in school come from backgrounds that differ from those of their students, there may be more support for learning in families than staff realise.

> **Bonus idea** ★
>
> When you have conversations with parents, try asking what they do to support learning in the home. This is best done anonymously (at the beginning, at least) – put up large sheets of paper and let people write answers during parents' evenings or concert nights.

Ladson-Billings, G. (2006), 'From the achievement gap to the education debt: Understanding achievement in US schools', *Educational Researcher*, 35, (7), 3–12.

Home learning environments matter – even for teenagers

'We try, Miss. We phone her up about her homework; we drop by to make sure she goes to school. But it's not the same as having your Mum care about you.' (A group of teenagers supporting a friend)

The literature is clear that what happens at home matters most. Students coming from what is termed a 'positive home learning environment' are more likely to succeed in schools.

What matters is what parents *do*. As a starting point, parents need to feel confident that they *can* help to support their children's learning and that this support can make a tangible difference. Some understandings of parental engagement stem from a flawed premise, assuming that what's important is parents' grasp of subject matter. That's not the case. Here's the difference: the *content* is learned in the classroom, while the home learning environment is about bringing the learning to life, *cementing* that knowledge and building *confidence* around learning.

What's important is the *attitude towards learning* in the home. Young people take their cue from their families; if parents believe that learning is important, young people will feel the same and, importantly, act on those feelings.

- It's vital to let parents know that they are still important to their children and their learning.
- Let parents know that mastering the content is not necessary for them to support learning. Offering a cup of tea, a quiet place to study and gentle encouragement matters.
- Reiterate to parents that they don't need to know the answers when assisting their children, but simply need to support the search.

Bonus idea ★

Share ideas from this book with parents, particularly about them not needing to master the content of what's taught in the classroom. Many parents can and have mastered that content and that's great – but they should never underestimate the value of just saying 'I'm proud of you' to their children.

Partnership working with parents

'We no longer see parental engagement as a separate thing – now, we just automatically think "Where do parents come into this?" for anything new we do.' (Governor)

Partnerships work best when they are built on a foundation of equality: equality of respect and equality of understanding. But equality doesn't mean sameness – nor does a good partnership necessitate that everyone does the same thing.

When we first started our research around parental engagement, staff often used the phrase 'singing from the same hymn sheet' to describe the relationship that they wanted from parents. We'd agree with this, but the difference is that it's not the school's hymn sheet – it's one that's created by the school together with families. And the end point of the hymn (if hymns can have end points) is the learning of the young person in common between the families and the school. That's the basis of the partnership between parents and school staff – that's the outcome that everyone is working towards.

For some parents, the current educational system can seem foreign and they may think that there is no point engaging with it. They may feel that they don't understand what is required of their children and doubt their own ability to support them effectively. Schools need to actively work to understand the value and meaning of *effective* parental engagement in young people's learning, and to share that understanding with parents. When the adults around them pull together and work collaboratively, young people have the best opportunity to thrive.

Teaching tip

In saying that schools should be working in partnership with parents, we are not saying that school staff and parents do the same thing – they most decidedly do not, and they shouldn't try to do the same things, although there are of course overlaps.

Taking it further

Spend some time in a meeting – staff, school, INSET or departmental – talking about what makes a good partnership, just in general. Now see how or if that can be applied to the way in which staff work with parents.

A wish-list for partnership

'Alone we can do so little, together we can do so much.' (Attributed to Helen Keller)

One of the problems that we've encountered in our work with schools is a lack of coordination between different members of staff, different sections of a school and even different events that may involve the same people.

Teaching tip

Ideally, parents would have had an input into what effective partnership with the school looks like ahead of any larger staff discussion. Compare what parents wish for to that desired by staff. Work hard to create a shared wish-list that focuses on how parents and teachers can support learning. There is a template wish-list in the online resources for this book.

A lot of schools have systems that allow them to text or message parents easily, and databases that hold information about parents. They may also have a desire to improve their relationships with parents, but all of these things have not been put together in a way that actually allows the final idea to happen. Yet it would be easy enough to pull all of these things together.

However, there is a more fundamental problem which is that often, actions in this area precede thought; a need is seen, and an event is put on to try to service that need (something must be done, here is something, therefore we will do it), but little thought is given to *how* the event will meet the need.

You wouldn't do that in your teaching – you'd spend more time thinking about what the need actually is and who has the need. Is it the whole class? Is it a few members of the class? Is it enough of the class to take time out of a class lesson or is there some other way?

It's the same with work with parents: to actually support their engagement with learning, you need to know what it is you're trying to do. That's one reason why we ask you to think about what you actually believe in Idea 10: What do we believe?

Create your 'wish-list for partnership' with parents. What do you want partnership with parents to look like? What do you hope that partnership will achieve?

- This is best done as a multi-step process; Rome wasn't built in a day nor will you be able to build a partnership with parents, or the groundwork for it, in one meeting.
- We'd suggest doing this as a group activity, perhaps at an INSET day (though include all members of staff who interact with parents).
- Get staff brainstorming that 'blue sky' thinking; don't worry about 'how' yet – just think about 'if'.
- Consider why the wish-list has yet to happen by surfacing any potential barriers (see Part 6). Be clear; saying 'funding' may well be true, but dig deeper – what is it you need funding *for*? – and consider whether there is any other way of accomplishing the same goal.
- Collectively consider how to overcome those barriers (see Part 6). (You're not at the planning stage yet – that comes later!) Be realistic, and see what can – and can't – be done.
- Now, and only now, start thinking about action: based on all of the above, what's reasonable to try to accomplish?

This process doesn't lead you to planning particular events – it should instead lead you to a place where you can begin that process, based on a solid understanding of what the outcomes of the process should be.

Bonus idea
Remember this is all about learning, and you have skills in this area. Approach these tasks as you approach any other learning task: think about outcomes, skills necessary, steps and stages.

Eyes on the prize: it's all about learning

'I didn't become a teacher to collect data, but that's all I seem to do.'

Throughout this book, we'll come back – again and again – to the fact that the really important thing about schools is facilitation of learning. After all, that's what schools exist for; the reason why we have schools in the first place is to ensure that our children have access to the learning that they need to function in society.

Taking it further

Meetings, especially, can take up valuable time that could be used to support learning directly or indirectly. We've all suffered through the 'meeting that should have been an email'. Think before calling meetings about whether they actually need to happen! That includes meetings with parents.

We're defining 'learning' quite broadly here – we don't mean just the hallowed 'three Rs' or even the things that will lead to the gold standard at GCSE, although those are, of course, important. Rather, we mean 'learning' to encompass not only the academic side of life but also the social side – after all, for many young people, school is the main place in which they learn to socialise with their peers.

For secondary students as well, school can be an entry into the world of work, with career days, placements and vocational learning running alongside numeracy and literacy (or better still, intertwined with them).

Here are some suggestions that can help with keeping this focus:

- Every meeting should begin and end with 'What does this have to do with learning?'
- Weigh time and effort against learning gains – if what you're doing doesn't support learning in some way, why are you spending so much time on it?

A whole-school effort

Part 2

What do we believe?

'Our beliefs shape our values, which in turn shape our vision.' (Headteacher)

Every school has a mission statement or vision – something that encapsulates what staff and students (and sometimes parents) believe about and want for the school.

Mission statements are often brightly decorated and hanging on walls throughout the school. They range, in our experience, from long, detailed and fulsome to short, snappy and sweet – with the latter being something like 'Learn! Be kind! Achieve!' and the former looking something akin to an early draft of *War and Peace*.

However, in our experience, this statement, which is supposed to cover the things that are important to the school community, rarely involves parents at any significant point. Schools are often good at 'talking the talk' and not so good at 'walking the walk'. In thinking about your own school's mission statement, you might want to think about how it was created – were parents involved?

- Does the statement mention parents or families at all?
- If parents weren't involved in the process, do parents even know that the statement exists, and if so (or if it's pointed out to them), do they agree with it?
- Do parents know how they can be involved in making the mission or vision a reality?

Writing a mission statement is not an easy task, and we don't want to suggest that every school needs to start again from scratch; if you've just finished rewriting yours as a school, for example, there are better uses of your time than going through all that again. However, if your statement is ready for renewal, we'd suggest the following:

- Share with parents *why* the school wants to work in an effective partnership with them (i.e. for the benefit of students' wellbeing and progress and to create alignment between approaches at home and school).
- Let families know about the process for writing the statement. Ensure that parents have a chance to contribute – not just through a questionnaire or a sheet sent home or just through parent governors (although these are all good starting places).
- Perhaps have meetings with parents just to talk about the mission statement; you'll have to judge what's best for your school community.
- If separate meetings are not possible, put up a poster about it with a suggestion box – located near to spots that parents will pass on parents' evenings, or somewhere they are likely to spend time, such as the tea and coffee tent.

When trying to convey to parents what you think effective partnership 'looks like', you could create a space on the website where parent partnership is celebrated. This may include video clips, for example – perhaps a short clip of something being taught that could be discussed at home. Indeed, in our experience, using a visual metaphor around partnership can efficiently convey what we ideally want to achieve together.

Taking it further

We've mentioned having an alignment between home and school, but that's not just a one-way process – be open to learning from parents!

Learning across the school

'What's this got to do with me? I'm not a pastoral manager, form tutor or the parent support officer. This isn't my job.'

Parental engagement needs to be a whole-school project. It's fine to have a champion but, particularly in a large secondary school, support for parental engagement in learning is too important to leave to one person.

Parental engagement is one of the best ways to support learning, so everyone who is ultimately interested in that learning (i.e. everyone in the school) needs to be interested in parental engagement. Obviously, some people will be more directly involved and in different ways: front-of-house staff, sports coaches, teachers and senior leaders all interact with parents but often in very different ways. It's important then, that there are shared understandings across the school about what is meant by parental engagement and how that is best accomplished in your particular setting with your parental cohorts.

- Ensure that everyone who interacts with parents has access to the same training – ideally, invite front-of-house staff, coaches, and so on, to any CPD relating to parental engagement.
- Ensure that supporting parental engagement is part of all staff meetings.
- If you have a staff bulletin board, post ideas for supporting parental engagement on the board and rotate them regularly.
- Have something about supporting parents as part of school and individual performance targets. This ensures that all staff know that the school takes the issue seriously. Targets should be clear, easily understood and measurable, for example, 'Positive phone calls with all parents in your form at least once a term' rather than 'Work to support parental engagement' (this is too vague).

Judge not...

'Our parents are tricky. Most of them just don't care.'

We keep emphasising the difference between parental *involvement* with school and parental *engagement* with learning because it's all too easy to judge parents as not involved or interested in learning on the basis of the wrong parameters.

What happens in the home learning environment is what impacts on young people's learning, and not what happens when parents come into school. School staff often underestimate what parents are doing with their children, understandably given the general lack of contact with parents in secondary schools. But there are always people ready to judge parents and their parenting – don't add to the chorus.

- Start with what your parents already do to support learning and go from there; take an asset-based approach.
- Transition into your school setting provides an optimal opportunity to find out about parental aspirations, family attitudes towards school and levels of confidence around supporting student learning.
- Try to remember how difficult it is for many parents to physically come to the school site at all. Some will have been to the school themselves as teenagers and will carry their own emotional baggage. Some may have overheard or been the recipients of comments like those at the start of this idea. Some will simply feel that teachers are far too scary to engage and communicate with. A genuine partnership with parents requires a level playing field, an understanding of 'who does what' in terms of supporting students and a sense that when difficulties arise, those conversations will take place in the spirit of partnership and cooperation.

Teaching tip

Don't make assumptions; just because you never or rarely see a parent doesn't mean that the family isn't engaged in supporting learning or that the parent 'doesn't care'.

Taking it further

Auditing parental feelings towards the school at the point of transition will identify parents who are feeling reticent about coming in. Create a video for the school website with a tour of the school, words of reassurance from an existing parent and the message that you are not there to judge, but to support.

Think beyond the classroom

'They never come in! How do we get them to come in?'

It's a mistake to think that learning only happens in the classroom – the old staple argument of 'if they're not in school, they're not learning' is clearly wrong. Young people also spend the majority of their time out of school – they're only in school for 15 to 25 per cent of their time.

For a long while, we've been using terminology inaccurately, contributing to some of the issues that we face around engaging parents in learning. We say 'education' and 'learning' when it would be far more accurate to say 'schooling'. Learning starts at birth and goes on throughout life – consider how much children learn before they even start nursery.

Therefore, it makes sense to think about what they are learning and how to support that learning when children are not in school.

- Subject matter content is probably best learned *or introduced* in the classroom.
- Classroom-based learning can be supported, deepened and extended outside school.
- Young people can increasingly do that themselves as they get older.
- However, as teachers already know, learning is an intensely social act – and that social action can easily involve family members.

Bonus idea ★

We know that learning is a social act – so why is so much homework supposed to be done alone? Occasionally set homework that enhances the quality of interaction between parent and student, meaning that students have to talk to family members, and parents have to play a role.

We're not suggesting that parents and other family members are substitutes for teachers – we're suggesting that all the adults around the young person have a role to play in supporting their learning. These roles are not the same, and no one would expect them to be. But that doesn't mean that one is more important than the other – the optimal situation for the young person is when everyone is working well together.

The importance of school leadership

'You manage things, you lead people.'
(Rear Admiral Grace Murray Hopper)

For many years, the research has been quite clear that any intervention around supporting parents and families is far more likely to be successful – and sustained – if it is led, or at least clearly supported, by senior leaders in the school.

This is simply common sense; by virtue of their positions in school, members of the senior leadership team (SLT) wield authority and influence. If you are a member of SLT, you can:

- Ensure that members of SLT not only attend training around parental engagement but are clearly enthusiastic and interested.
- Ensure that supporting parental engagement is part of the school development plan and enshrined in staff targets, as appropriate to people's roles and responsibilities.
- Be conscious of how important a role model you are to other members of staff in terms of how you interact with parents daily.
- Be conscious of the language used to describe parents, and experiences with parents, throughout the school. Make sure that it is positive and truly denotes the manner in which you would talk about a genuine 'partner'.

If you are not a member of SLT:

- Suggest the points above, asking for supporting parental engagement to be one of your yearly targets – and ask for appropriate support to meet that target.
- If you're asked what subjects would be useful to cover in CPD or INSET days, you know what to suggest!

Teaching tip

It's worth noting that we want the quote at the outset of this idea, about leading and managing, to apply to your work with parents as well as with other staff at school!

Taking it further

There is a list of recommended reading about school leadership in the online resources for this book.

Bonus idea

One of the greatest examples of school leadership that we have witnessed was seeing a much-revered headteacher sitting outside the school in a rainy bus stop with a very nervous and vulnerable parent. She didn't demand that the parent come to her big, scary office, but instead met her informally and chose to have the difficult chat there.

Ditch the school improvement plan

'It's rather like building a very good transport system that crosses a continent, but stops a mile short of the final station. SIPs are aiming at the wrong end point: school improvement is not a goal; it's a step on the way to a goal, and that goal is the improvement of learning.' (Janet Goodall)

For some time now, we've been advocating that schools should change their school improvement plan (SIP) to a 'learning improvement plan'. After all, the end product of an SIP *is* the improvement of learning, isn't it?

Teaching tip

Of course, we're going to say that this process not only needs to include family members but also needs to highlight the place of parental engagement with learning throughout – after all, it's all about learning!

The only way to improve the school is to improve the learning going on in the school (and bear in mind that we don't mean only the learning that the students are doing – we mean 'learning' as inclusively as possible, to include student learning, teacher learning and the learning undertaken by other staff and, most certainly, by parents).

Of course, we are not suggesting a simple change to the title of the SIP, with the plan itself remaining the same. Rather, we're suggesting here (as elsewhere) a fairly full-scale overhaul of the thinking around what happens in school. We're suggesting a radical change, in the high old sense of the word 'radical', which comes from the Latin meaning 'root'.

And that means asking some basic questions – questions that we all thought about early on in our careers, but often haven't had the time to address since then. We'd suggest, if possible, that these questions form a continuing part of school meetings (and governors' meetings as well!). The questions are also useful to discuss with parents and, indeed, with students; their answers might surprise you.

- What is school for, overall? We spend a remarkable amount of time and effort making the school as good as it can be – but what are we trying to make it good *at*? This isn't a question about how the school will be judged by outsiders (league tables, Ofsted or Estyn, and so on) but rather a question about what you, as members of a school community, think that it should be doing – and why.
- How does your school fit into that? What, specifically, is your school for? Who is it for?
- Having decided what school is for, how are you going to get from where you are now to where you want to be?

Now that you hopefully have some answers to those questions, you can start to make a learning improvement plan (or replace 'learning' with the appropriate word for your school).

Bonus idea

Even if you can't follow through on all of these suggestions, simply try changing the 'school improvement plan' to the 'Name of School improvement plan' – that can sometimes make enough of a difference to show what's important to your school, rather than just what's generically important.

Support support staff

'Hello, and thank you for calling our school. How can I help you?'
(Often the first words a parent hears when contacting a school...)

The results from research in the field, along with our own experience, make it clear that staff are often poorly supported in relation to working with parents.

Teaching tip

You'll notice that we frequently talk about 'school staff' where you might expect us to say 'teachers'. That's a deliberate choice, because so many people who are not teachers engage with parents, right alongside teaching staff.

It is unusual, to say the least, for initial teacher training to touch on parents in more than a cursory way; it is often left to the students' mentors in schools to supply information about engaging with parents. Moreover, there is often little support in relation to working with parents once teachers are in place, particularly in secondary schools, where the emphasis is far more likely to be on subject knowledge and the teaching (and assessment) of particular content.

This seems manifestly unfair to us: we are asking teaching and other staff to take on incredibly important duties without adequate support or training. This idea is thus aimed particularly at those who can influence training and support for staff. That doesn't, however, limit this tip to the senior leadership team; any teacher who works with other teachers or with teaching assistants (who often have more interaction with parents than teaching staff, particularly if the teaching assistants live in the community and the teachers do not) is in a position of influence. Those who act as mentors to newly qualified teachers are in a position to support learning with regard to the value and realities of parental engagement (what it really is and how to best support it for the families in that particular school). And, of course, we are also aiming this idea at members of the leadership team of the school, whether middle leaders (head of department,

head of year or head of subject) or at more
senior levels.

- Parental engagement in children's learning
  is one of the better ways of tackling the
  achievement gap or educational debt: it's
  important to ensure that all staff are aware
  of how important it is and have access to the
  best research in the area.
- Look at the list of employees in the school
  and, next to each name or role, note how
  and when they might interact with parents
  and what support they might need to do that
  well or better. Check this list with staff.
- As far as possible, include all staff in training
  related to working with parents; if that's not
  possible, arrange separate training for those
  who come into contact with parents most
  often, especially front-of-house staff, such as
  those working in reception.
- Also show these staff how important their job
  is in relation to parents and families, and how
  much it's valued by the school.

Taking it further

We've noted you don't
need to do everything
from scratch. If your
school works with other
schools, such as feeder
schools, ask them about
any training they are
having around parental
engagement. See if you
can set up joint training
– that will help ensure
that parents have a clear,
consistent message from
all parties!

The perils of policy (borrowing)

'That's all very well for you, but it wouldn't work in our school.'

Most teachers have had the experience of walking out of a lesson thinking, 'That didn't work — why not? It's always worked before!' One of the main reasons why the same lesson doesn't always work in the same way is simply that there are different students every time we teach it. What works for one group may not work, or may work differently, with another group.

The same is true of almost everything, of course, and work around supporting parental engagement is no different. Threaded throughout this book are suggestions for thinking outside the box, working with other schools and learning from the wider world. But they come with a caveat: not everything will work everywhere.

It's important to look beyond what your individual school 'has always done' to find new ideas and inspiration, but these ideas need to be considered in light of the reality in which your school lives. To adapt ideas from elsewhere, you need to know your setting well, just as you need to know your students well to adapt lessons to help them learn. Use data from your parent or family audit to help you know what will support your parents. The people who are best placed to tell you what will help your parents are the parents themselves. Before planning anything, talk to parents to find out what they want and need. Make it easy for them to get this information to you.

Teaching tip

Remember that you already have many of the skills needed to support parental engagement. You often pick up ideas and materials and apply them to your own classes, and the process of picking up ideas about supporting parents is the same.

Bonus idea ★

Place a suggestion box, paper and pens wherever parents are likely to be – such as the hall during parents' evening – to find out what parents want. Include a poster nearby to say what has been done in relation to the suggestions already received.

Change the discourse

'I'll forget what you tell me but I'll remember the way you make me feel.'

Our ideas are shaped not only by our experiences but also by what we hear, the conversations around us and even the posters we see every day.

A random internet search for motivational posters found such gems as 'Just choose to succeed!' and even 'Poverty draws a line – choose to step over it!' The underlying message here is the idea that success, happiness and even overcoming poverty are personal choices. To some extent, of course, this is true, but in a very real sense it's not only untrue but also delivers an insidious and dangerous message: that systemic issues (such as poverty, austerity, discrimination, and so on) can be overcome by personal choice – and of course they can't.

This is a complex issue that we can't cover completely here; we'd just like to suggest some things to think about.

- The 'discourse of poverty' is a term used for the idea that all people experiencing poverty have the same ideas, experiences and aspirations. It's nonsense, of course, but the idea is pervasive. We need to ensure that it's not colouring our thinking about parents and families.
- Don't set parents up to fail by asking them to participate in activities that mean their economic situation is highlighted inadvertently (such as dressing up for World Book Day).
- Consider staff sharing their own 'overcoming' stories visibly, to empower and support parents. It can be incredibly powerful to find out that a teacher has come from the same background or set of challenging situations. More importantly, it means that parents might feel less judged when opening up about challenges they might be facing.

Teaching tip

Consider for a moment the way a parent who is struggling to feed, clothe and house her family feels when told, 'Just choose to step over the line of poverty!'

Bonus idea ★

Try replacing 'child', 'student', 'pupil' and 'parent' in your conversation and writing for a day, just using 'person' or 'people'. How does that change what you're saying and what it means?

Model learning and let parents know

'Those teachers – they think they know it all and then they come and tell us.'

Our constant experience as teachers and trainers is that teachers are amazingly open to new learning (which makes sense when you think about it).

Teaching tip

In sharing materials, make sure that you abide by copyright. Ensure that it's OK to copy or distribute materials.

Even better is that the world obliges: there are constant – and increasing – opportunities for CPD for teaching staff, even as the time and finances available to them seem to shrink in proportion. In this idea, we want to give you some suggestions for useful, practical CPD that doesn't cost the earth, but we also want to suggest that you share the work you are doing with parents.

Here are some ideas for CPD that you could try:

- Use this book! Get together with colleagues – within your school or, even better, across schools – and discuss the ideas in this book (as a starting point rather than an end point!). What worked? What didn't, and how do you know? What needs to be adapted for your situation and why? How could you do it?
- Have a dedicated space – physical and digital – for staff to share materials, particularly from training that they have attended. Make sure that there's an easy-to-use guide or index – otherwise, the store of materials will never be used because no one will be able to find anything! Just have a simple form asking for a line or two of description of the materials as they are deposited. Make sure that everyone knows where the materials are and how to access them.
- Create a group of like-minded colleagues to investigate a given idea – say one a term.

Make the group meetings pleasant (local pub, cafe or park perhaps?) so that people want to attend.

- The amount of research on any given topic is very likely to be daunting – you simply can't read it all. Find a few things that look interesting and spread them around the group. Not everyone needs to read everything – you can share the information.
- Alternatively, pick one thing and everyone reads it – a bit like a book or journal club.

Having done one or more of the above, we'd suggest that you share it with parents (or, if appropriate, invite parents along). This shows parents:

- that you are still learning. It models for them that you don't know everything, and that when you ask them to learn something new, they're not alone.
- what you are learning or thinking about **and** how it relates to their children. For example: 'We're closed on Monday for an INSET day, to help us be better able to teach the new curriculum' or 'Mrs Jones will be away next week as she's on a course about the Great Fire of London, which is a big topic in the history A level. We're looking forward to her sharing some of the photos from the course in the next newsletter!'

Taking it further

Make sure that you keep records of any of the professional development you do, even if it's not 'formal' (classes or INSET days). It's still all part of growing the profession and developing yourself as a professional.

Beware the power-play

'The master's tools will never dismantle the master's house.'
(Audre Lorde)

Parents may feel scared of teachers, with such fears stemming from experiences in their own education or a genuine belief that teachers are intellectually superior and potentially judgemental.

We are aware of one secondary school that informed parents during the very first 'meet and greet' to stay back, not interfere or question how children were progressing in their learning, and generally leave things to the 'experts'. Such assertions set the wrong tone from the beginning and devalue parental engagement, cutting off an important means of support for student learning from the get-go. The opportunity for the school to learn more about individual students is also lost and important information not passed on. Who would dare to challenge the scary headteacher?

Parents' fears may be unfounded in your school, but what can you do to alleviate such fears?

- Build rapport with parents at the first opportunity (transition always provides a fruitful point at which staff can convey warmth, rapport and commonalities with families).
- Use plain language with parents; they don't need to use school terms or words that require pedagogical knowledge.
- Ensure that parents know they should always feel comfortable to ask questions, no matter how basic.
- Collate 'FAQs' that parents ask the school every year; these can perhaps live on the school website and be easily accessible to parents. This sets a healthy, transparent tone that suggests they aren't the first parent to ask that question. It can be edited as and when new questions get submitted.

PTA, parent council, parent forum... use your groups

'Parent groups aren't just about raising money anymore.'

You almost certainly already have some, perhaps many, groups with parents as members in your school, including a PTA, parent council or perhaps parent forum, particularly in Scotland.

PTAs may traditionally have been about raising funds but are now moving towards being more involved in the life of the school and particularly in the lives of families. One issue with many of these groups, however, is that often they are composed of 'the same people over and over again'. In actual fact, the groups will be composed of those parents (usually mothers) who feel comfortable coming into school, and who have the time and self-confidence to do so and to be involved in organised groups.

We remember one headteacher who carefully set up a room for a new parent group they wanted to start, with pads of paper and pens set out at places around a boardroom table. Ten parents came in, and nine immediately turned around and left; those parents had no experience of that type of set-up (or had only had bad experiences in such rooms!).

None of this means that the parent groups you already have should be abandoned or aren't of value – in fact, one complaint we've heard from parents is that the ones who are 'always at the school' often feel undervalued, as there's so much emphasis on reaching the others! Instead, start with what you have and work from there. Make sure you ask your current parent groups what they want – from the school and from their children's schooling.

Teaching tip

In secondary schools, it can be harder for parents to make the sorts of connections that can occur naturally in the primary playground – you may have to engineer places and times for parents to come together.

Bonus idea ★

We'll say this a number of times, but never underestimate the value of tea, coffee, biscuits and cakes – or a full meal, if you can. People are social animals but often need something simple to root them to one spot for more than a minute or two – tea is a good starter!

Old skills, new uses

'I don't know how to work with parents; no one's ever trained me to do that!'

One of the ideas we've reiterated throughout this book is that while some new skills are needed for supporting parents, you already have the basic skills.

Think about a typical day in the classroom. How often do you support a student who lacks confidence, help a student overcome barriers, stretch a student, encourage a student who is struggling, or use phrases, such as 'No, you can't do it *yet*, but you will be able to'? Now relate these to parents:

- Many parents lack confidence in their ability to help their children learn at this level.
- Many parents face barriers to engaging with their children's learning and with the school.
- Many parents are already doing plenty to support learning but want to do more and just don't know how or what to do.
- Many parents struggle for a number of reasons when it comes to engaging with their children's learning.
- Many parents may have given up on supporting learning in the home after bad experiences, either with their own schooling or with their children's school(s).

Students in secondary schools are often referred to as 'young adults', after all. We'd suggest that the switch between supporting the learning of Early Years pupils and their parents is much greater than that between supporting the learning of secondary students and theirs. We're not suggesting that you treat parents in the same way you treat students! We are, however, suggesting that many of the skills you need to support parents are already there – you've been honing them for years.

What's special about secondary?

Part 3

What's different about this phase?

'Parental engagement matters just as much in secondary school, yet parents just don't get that.' (Deputy head)

We wrote this second book about parental engagement because staff working in secondary schools asked us to, pointing to the many differences in the two phases of education.

Some of the issues that secondary teachers have mentioned to us include:

- Children are taught by a range of teachers.
- Security is often tighter in secondary schools, making parents even more intimidated by the prospect of coming into school.
- The nature of secondary schools – larger, more complex, with so many more staff to interact with – is off-putting for many parents.
- Contacting parents is often different in secondary school, particularly as many young people will make their own way to and from school. The chance of 'catching' a parent at home time or the start of the day is much slimmer than in primary, meaning that interactions with parents are often more formal, more planned and less regular.
- Parents of young people in secondary school often have less contact with other parents and are less likely to know their children's friends (and their parents), meaning that many parents lose a support mechanism as their children go into secondary school.
- Catchment areas for secondary schools are generally larger than those for primary schools, so parents are also more geographically spread out.

Parental engagement in learning changes as children age but absolutely still matters.

What does 'parent' mean for secondary students?

'On the one hand he wants cuddles, yet on the other, he tells me I really embarrass him!' (Mum with 13-year-old son)

Anyone with children knows that your relationship with them changes as they grow – seemingly day to day at times.

One day, you're carefully ensuring that they don't fall over as they start to walk, and the next you're asking for the car keys back...

- Adolescence is a time of constant negotiation of boundaries, freedoms and new ideas.
- Starting secondary school can be frightening for young people and parents alike; the more you can do to alleviate anxiety, the better.
- Parents of secondary students may feel that they can't 'help' with schoolwork because the content is new to them or because school at this level has changed too much.
- Young people have told researchers that what they want most from their parents is moral support, approbation and guidance.
- It's important that young people are asked how they are getting on (even if they never answer!).

As we mentioned in the introduction, it's important to remember that 'parent', as we're using it in this book, can mean many people other than just biological parents. We define 'parent' to mean 'any adult with a caring responsibility for the young person'. Increasingly, young people are being looked after by grandparents, and have been in such relationships since they started school. Not all young people are in a family situation and not everyone is in a 'traditional' family.

Teaching tip

For teenagers, the pool of people in a caring relationship may widen to include others such as youth group leaders and sports coaches. It's important to know who these people are for individual students (and to know, and record and use as appropriate, who has a legal responsibility for the young person).

Taking it further

Try saying 'make sure someone at home sees or signs this' rather than 'make sure mum sees this', a phrase that might unwittingly upset a student. Don't make assumptions about the nature of any student's family set-up.

All parents, not just the usual few

'Oh, you know the type of parents who are here all the time – you can always count on them!'

Every teacher knows about the different sorts of parents that they encounter, and one group consists of those parents who are very happy to be in school. They attend every fete, they are the backbone of the PTA and the governing body, and they can always be called upon to help out when needed.

Teaching tip

Make sure that you thank the 'parents who are always there' – show how much you appreciate the work they do for you and for all the young people in the school.

These parents are often vital to the running of a school, particularly in times when school finances are so tight. They are usually parents who are comfortable in the school setting, often people for whom schooling was an enjoyable experience, and often people who come from backgrounds similar to those of the teaching staff. These are very important people in any school, and it's important to acknowledge that.

However, it's *also* important not to use these parents as a model for all parents (or even as a model to which all parents should aspire). It's important not to assume that these parents are more engaged in learning than those parents who don't come to school as often – or those who don't come at all. This takes us back to the distinction that we made previously between parental *involvement* with the school (which is important and is what these parents are showing) and parental *engagement* in learning (which is vital, and which is rarely directly seen by teaching staff).

One consequence of considering these parents (and we are often taken aback by staff who refer to 'parents' almost as a different species when they themselves are parents...) as models of all parents is that anything put on for this group will be tailored to it – and quite possibly not tailored to, or useful for, other groups of parents.

Research has shown a worrying fact: work to support parental engagement in learning which targets only those parents who are already comfortable coming into school and comfortable with school staff, can quite possibly *widen* the gap between students from different economic backgrounds. It can give more advantage to those who are already advantaged, rather than supporting those most in need of support.

- Remember that other people in the school are parents as well – front-of-house staff, staff working in kitchens and libraries, groundskeepers, coaches, and so on. Think widely when you think of 'parents'.
- Ask the parents who are comfortable coming into school to bring another parent with them to a school event – often it's easier to come to something with someone you know, rather than just on your own.
- Don't neglect the parents who are 'always around' – ask their opinions and get their take on newsletters. Their input is very valuable; just make sure that they are not the only parents you ask.

Bonus idea

School leaders, remember that many of your staff are parents as well. Ensure they get the time they need to support their own children and attend fetes, science fairs and parents' evenings.

The importance of parental self-efficacy

'I realised that I *am* a good parent, and that I *can* do a good job.'

At the core of positive parental engagement with children's learning is a parent's *belief in their ability to help their own child*.

Often, well-educated parents find it easier to have that confidence than parents who have not enjoyed the same exposure to education. When parents feel empowered and knowledgeable, when they *know* they can help, they are more likely to engage. Parents can be fearful of interfering with what school is doing, confusing their children or even teaching them the wrong thing (based on what they consider to be outdated knowledge). You can support parental self-efficacy by:

- Allowing parents to see what the learning outcomes are per subject, per term. Show them what they can do to support learning.
- Delving into the parent pool at school when you require expertise. Perhaps you are running a science week and know that there is an engineer parent or scientist grandparent. Ask them whether they can participate in science week.
- Showing parents how parental input can shape outcomes.
- Asking parents what they *already* do to support learning. Remember that this is a two-way process. It's not just about school staff *telling* parents; it's also about school staff *listening* to parents.
- Sending letters home to parents of children who are showing promise academically, praising the support that the students have received at home.

The importance of parent-to-parent work

'That's the thing – in primary you knew all the other parents; in secondary, I don't know any of them.'

You will be aware of the concept of peer coaching among students and staff, and how beneficial such work can be. Equally, new parents can greatly benefit from the wisdom and knowledge of those who have gone before them. There is value in not feeling alone...

Parents can take new parents on school tours, answering questions about how things work and passing on tips you hadn't even thought about. Indeed, some parents prefer to talk to other parents. Parents of older students in the school can help new parents understand changes to exams, assessments and curriculum, passing on the information as it affects parents and families. There are usually some confident parents who are happy to fulfil this role.

- Peer-to-peer support between parents has been shown to be very effective and supportive, but may not happen by chance, particularly at secondary – as we've seen, parents are unlikely to meet at the school gate, for example.
- There are many ways of facilitating parents mixing with each other: shared meals are often a good way to break the ice. Some schools use 'pot luck dinners' where every family brings something to share as a starter.
- If you do work with parent champions, be sure that they are representative of the parent body as a whole, not just the 'parents who are always around'. Seek out parents you know are already supporting learning at home, even if they don't come into school all that often – start the conversation by showing that you appreciate the work they are doing.

Taking it further

Consider a formal coaching scheme for parents where 'newbie parents' are given an allocated parent mentor to show them the ropes. Remember to evaluate it if you do put such a scheme in place. Consider parental confidence, as that is what matters most!

Working together across subjects

'It's all so bitty in secondary school – I can't keep track of it all! Primary was a lot easier.'

One of the things that's quite clear from the research, as well as from our work with families, is that a lack of consistency across the school is very confusing for parents.

Taking it further

Research has shown that teachers rate talking to other teachers as the best form of CPD. Try to ensure that teachers have the space and time to do this – it may need to be engineered into INSET days just by having longer breaks and lunchtimes!

This doesn't mean that every subject has to do the same thing. For example, if the French department is sending home postcards to praise good work, that doesn't mean that the English department also has to send postcards, particularly if they have a different use for that budget (such as attending a performance of a play on the A level syllabus). However, what *is* important is that parents know what each department is doing – otherwise, parents might easily (and understandably) get the idea that their child is doing well in French and not in English (due to a lack of postcards).

- It's important that different groups of teachers know what's going on in different parts of the school – at least in outline form – so that they can answer parents' questions or direct those questions to the right person.
- See Idea 46 for our recommendation of a database to share ideas and materials – this should be easy to consult.
- Sharing what each department or faculty is doing is also a way of sharing good practice.

Remember that if you have a vision for working with parents that has been articulated and created by all staff, with input from parents, it is highly likely that consistent approaches to parent–school partnership will be in place and valued.

Working with feeder schools

'It makes so much sense for us to work closely with our feeder schools. It alleviates problems in the long run.'
(Secondary headteacher)

In our work with schools, one thing that we have noticed time and time again is the lack of sharing good practice and great ideas between schools. This is often down to not having enough time to get together or having someone to organise this.

We argue that it's not only important but it's vital that schools share information, not just about the students who will be arriving in the new school year, but also about the context from which they will arrive (and to which they will return at the end of every day).

We are certainly not asking teachers to gossip about families; we are, however, saying that, as professionals, there is information that teachers in feeder primary schools have that is important to share with their secondary colleagues.

- We've found that there can be wariness between teachers from different phases: primary teachers worry they don't have enough subject knowledge; secondary teachers worry they can't be generalists.
- We've also found that when teachers from different phases actually have the chance to work together, amazing things can happen.
- This is because they share an overarching concern: the learning of the young people they work with.
- Primary staff may also be in a position to collate information from students and their families about their aspirations for their time at secondary school. Referring to this information can be very meaningful for students and their families on entry to secondary, knowing that the new teachers care just as much as the former ones.

Teaching tip

We've mentioned the fine line between gossip and information. When exchanging information about children and families, ask a simple question: is this the sort of information that you would like exchanged about your family? Or how would the parents in question feel if they heard what was said?

It's not a matter of money

'We realised that we can do a lot of stuff ourselves. We don't need an educational consultant to come in.'

Sometimes, ideas are understandably not taken on board because a lack of money means that other things must be prioritised. If you are trying to drive parental engagement, the good news is that your school doesn't have to be well-resourced financially.

Taking it further

Parents have jobs, connections, links to other organisations, stories to tell, skills to contribute and resources to offer your school. By knowing your parent community, you are better able to dip into that resource pool as and when you need it. Parents welcome being asked.

The majority of this book's ideas can be implemented easily and cost-effectively to good effect, because parental engagement is about a tone that you might use in your conversations with parents or an image that you use to convey the idea of partnership, and is genuinely driven by mutual care and a desire to see a student thrive.

Parents are there as a resource to help and support young people's learning, their great power often yet to be unleashed. Parent partnership is about an investment in the relationship at all stages. Establishing rapport and connection and setting the tone early are all free to do and mean that a school is proactively working to ensure that parents are seen and felt to be genuine partners.

There are a number of free tools out there that you can use to measure and audit parental feelings, attitudes and opinions on all matters relating to learning. Parents like to be asked their view; it makes them feel valued. Parents want to know that you are striving to work with them, even if you don't always get it right. The bottom line is that you don't need to do all the heavy lifting. Parental partnership is about the relationship, and about what is not tangible or easily measured but worth every penny of time. But be sure you close the feedback loop and let parents know what you've done in response to their comments!

Reporting back to parents

'I never read his school report; it just sits in the drawer.'

It's amazing to think that you might put all that effort into writing and composing a school report and parents don't even read it.

One reason why is that they might assume it is written for the students rather than the parents. Another obstacle is the language used within it: secondary schools might talk about 'levels', 'predicted grades' or 'below-average progress', or use acronyms that are completely meaningless to parents. Before you write a report, remember that parents want to know:

- you know and value their child
- you appreciate the child's potential and are working to help nurture it
- you appreciate all the positives but want to work with the student and parents to help the student where they may be struggling.

These ideas may help:

- Never say that a student has an issue without suggesting ways in which parents can help! It is fruitless for parents to hear that Jessica never puts her hand up in class without receiving some ideas for how they can help.
- Reports can sometimes aggravate parents unnecessarily through inaccessible language, an unhelpful tone, relaying information that parents would have liked to have known earlier or by only talking only about the struggles and never where the student has thrived.
- Parents are more likely to read a school report when it is electronically accessible and there isn't a report to print out. The beauty of e-reports is that you can use hyperlinks to signpost students and parents to useful revision videos for subjects where children are struggling, for example.

Teaching tip

If you do use e-reports, ensure that they are optimised for reading on a phone and that there is another option for parents who can't access the report in this way.

Taking it further

The skills you already have can help you – approach writing a report like you approach any other learning situation. What's the outcome? How are you going to help the parent get there?

Reporting to support

'They're rubbish – you don't find out anything you didn't already know.' (Parent on parents' evenings)

For many years, we've been asking teachers how they – as parents to their own children – feel about the parents' evenings that they attend. The quote above is typical of the responses we receive; we rarely find anyone who (as a parent) thinks that these events are fit for purpose.

Teaching tip

Approach parents' evening like any other learning activity. What do you want to achieve from it? What's the outcome, and how are you going to get there?

Taking it further

Make sure that parents have an idea of what teachers look like before they come to parents' evening, and have a map telling them where teachers will be located. This will make the evening run more smoothly.

But still, year in and year out, we continue the same old process – a process that adds considerably to teachers' workloads, is often highly inconvenient for parents and tends to be very stressful for everyone involved.

You've almost certainly sent home a report about how the child is doing, and so simply telling parents what they already know from the report is pretty much a waste of everyone's time. There are, however, a few pointers that should help to improve the meetings from everyone's perspective.

- Try configuring your parents' meetings around the future and not the past. What can the parent or young person do to improve? How can parents help?
- Ask parents things, and don't just tell them things. Ask them what they want to know (preferably before the meeting, so that you can come prepared).
- Ask parents what they can tell you about their child that will help you to help the child learn.
- Remember that, for a lot of parents, if their child is doing well in school, the parents' evening is the *only* time when anyone ever tells them that.
- Tell parents good things as well as those things that are bad or problematic.

- Tell parents that they are doing a good job, and find examples if you can to show this. Generally, no one ever tells parents that they are doing well, yet the vast majority of people turn out OK!
- If you are a parent yourself, think about what you would want your child's teachers to tell you – and build your meetings around that.
- If you are a member of SLT (or can influence one), think about asking parents what they want at parents' meetings and then see what you can do about meeting those requests.
- Remember that a lot of parents are frightened of coming into school, based on their own experiences. You are trying to repair bridges that other people have broken. Setting out terrifying books with incomprehensible data, sitting across from (rather than alongside) parents, using teacher-speak – all of these make the experience worse, rather than better, for parents.

Bonus idea

Never underestimate the value of tea, coffee and biscuits at parents' evenings – and make sure that teachers are kept supplied as well!

Understanding the parents of teenagers

Part 4

Parenting is different for teenagers – but still vital

'Parents have a lot on their plates these days. We need to make sure that the messages we are giving at school are being echoed at home.' (Headteacher)

Parenting is hard. Today's parents often work outside the home and are extremely busy trying to support their families. What all parents have in common, however, is a hope that their children will not end up taking risks that compromise their health and happiness.

Teaching tip

Remember that each family is different; parents will have their own set of cultural, social and religious values that will influence responses to most PSHE topics. However, if schools can play a role in prompting family discussion and in getting families to reflect on family values with their teens, it is a promising start.

Somewhat encouragingly, recent data published by the Health Behaviours in School-Aged Children Survey (2020) suggests that our teens are taking fewer drugs, smoking less and engaging in less sexually risky behaviour than in previous years.

When schools are working in partnership with families, teens have an optimal chance to thrive during these challenging years. PSHE lessons in school are a good start, but when parents are encouraged to convey *evidence-based* messages to their children and are supported by their schools in terms of *how* to do that, such partnership working can really help teens.

- Ensure that parents are aware of the messages that you are trying to convey to teens in PSHE lessons, but keep it simple. They don't need a copy of the curriculum or your lesson plan, but they do need to know the 'gist' so that they can mirror the messages that you are trying to convey in class.
- Try to engage parents alongside teens in thinking about some of these topics within family time. Kitchen table discussions might be kick-started by questions such as:

Why might a teen start vaping? How difficult is it to resist peer pressure? Should particular drugs be decriminalised or not? Can you help parents to initiate such conversations within family life?

- Try to make any work in this area very context-specific. You might send home a case study for teens to discuss with their wider family that involves a scenario common to teens. Perhaps they have to discuss choices available to the teen, parental responses to that choice, consequences following each choice and optimal outcomes. Perhaps you can help parents to scaffold the conversation with their teen by providing a few conversational prompts that accompany the case study. This is truly parental engagement in action, with the school playing a fundamental role in enriching the quality of interaction between parents and teenagers in relation to some of the most important issues.

Taking it further

You might frame homework in terms of debates teens could have with their parents or you could embark on project work that covers this ground and that sparks 'family talk'.

Transitioning transition

'It's like having the security blanket taken away – or the rug yanked out from under you.' (How some parents have described the move from primary to secondary school)

It's worth remembering that parents are also a part of transition; they are having to get used to new ideas and ways of working with a school, along with supporting all the changes their children are experiencing.

Taking it further

Parent-to-parent work has been shown to be remarkably effective. Asking current parents to be around when new parents visit the school and to give input on what being a parent of a secondary student is like would be very helpful.

Transition is a time of great change for students, in all sorts of ways – as you know well. On a practical level, they are in a new setting, which is usually much larger than the one they are used to, with far more people to get to know. They've moved from usually having one teacher and staying in one room all day to having a number of teachers and moving around a new building multiple times a day. On a personal level, they've gone from being the oldest in the primary school to being the youngest in a secondary – often experiencing not only physical but also mental and emotional disorientation along the way (not to mention all the other upheavals that come with puberty).

We have noticed that some parents assume their job around learning is done when their children arrive at secondary school. If schools set the tone that parents are surplus to requirements and all children are now expected to be independent, parental disengagement can become the acceptable norm. Transition is an important time to:

- Set the tone. Clearly let parents know how important their role is in terms of supporting their children over the coming academic year. What might this support look like?
- Show that you care about questions that parents may have (no matter how basic). Ask

current Year 8 parents what they wish they had known; better still, work with them to create a new parents' handbook or update the one that already exists. E-books on the website work well.

- Ensure that parents know how to contact staff and understand response times (for example, you will receive a response within 48 hours or two working days).
- Make it clear which areas of the school parents are allowed to physically access or not and during what times. If some areas are restricted (lab or technical areas with potentially dangerous equipment), tell parents why.
- Make it clear 'who's who' in the school, so that parents know who to contact in different circumstances. New students may benefit from seeing pictures of their new subject teachers in advance of the school start (familiarity helps!). During that first day, if they are able to recognise a teacher, it helps to ease those early nerves.
- Establish security measures for getting into school. What will happen when parents come onto the school site? Are they required to sign in? Will they have to wear a badge? Let parents know why these measures are in place – it's for the safety of everyone in school: young people, staff and visitors.
- Make a little video to show them around the school website. This is where you can find information (show them the drop-down menus, for example). Get a current parent to make the video for you. They don't even need to appear on camera!
- A video can be created for parents and prospective parents showing a typical day in school. This is an ideal format because it can be watched again and again, year on year, and doesn't cost much to produce.
- When you are thinking about making and signposting audio-visual resources, plan the content alongside parents and students.
- Provide information about the VLE (virtual learning environment), if one is being used.

Bonus idea ★
Break down barriers at the first parent meeting. Use name tags that say something about the person wearing them: 'I'm Mr Henderson, ask me about history!' If school staff are known by honorifics (Mr, Miss, Sir…) then extend the same courtesy to parents.

Working parents = tired parents

'The school insisted I come in for a chat after school. I lost my day's wages – why can't they just video call me?'

Working parents love their children as much as any other parent, but they are time-poor.

We have enormous sympathy for parents who work day jobs and even night shifts, and who are still expected to help children with homework, be there for every school event and workshop and be able to communicate effectively with the school. It is very, very hard. So when you do call on them, take care to consider the following.

- Be sure that you know an optimal time to call or email.
- When you want them to come into the school, ensure that it is for a very good reason, and give plenty of notice.
- Where you can, use technology to initiate chats. Wouldn't they rather talk to you after a long day from the comfort of their armchair with a cup of tea in their hand, rather than have to get ready after work and make their way into school?
- Remember that parents can feel very guilty about working and not being able to support their children as much as they want to. Don't add to this. Enquire and take an interest in the parents' work where appropriate. Those informal chats about work can ease trickier, more difficult conversations later on.
- Think about yourself and how you feel if you are a parent – put yourself in their place!

Parents of young people with additional needs

'I am in and out of the school every week, sometimes twice a week. It is exhausting.'

When a child has special educational needs, parents can spend a great deal of time engaging with teachers, schools and other professionals. Often they can feel isolated because they spend so much time gathering information and seeking help, and may be called into school more than other parents.

Parent–teacher partnership can be critical for students to reach their potential. Parents of students with SEN are generally highly knowledgeable about their own children, what motivates or demotivates them and what circumstances might trigger particular responses.

- Always consider the parent the 'expert' on their child and seek their advice on how best to support the young person.
- Show that you are willing to learn. You may not have had training on managing particular conditions, but parents will appreciate you wanting to understand and learn more.
- When sharing information with the parent, adopt a tone of exploration and partnership: 'I have noticed this... Have you noticed anything? What do you think we can do to lessen their anxiety in the canteen?'
- SEN students and their families are some of the most resilient and extraordinary people out there. Schools need to make sure that this is recognised. For example, prize-giving ceremonies should not only be about academic achievement but also celebrate ways in which all students contribute to the school community. Do you value students' perseverance, kindness and personal resilience? Schools need to be inclusive in all approaches.

Teaching tip

Parents of SEN children tend to welcome compassion, understanding and knowing that you care. Many will feel conscious that they are taking up a lot of your time, and need to be told that you don't mind.

Bonus idea ★

We understand why schools have attendance awards. But some students will never be able to win such an award due to health issues (or those of a carer or parent). Think about what you as a school can do about showing appreciation in other ways.

Are teachers human?

'I ran into the teacher in Asda – I was amazed! I didn't realise they shopped there!'

Many teachers have had the experience of meeting a student or parent out of place, as it were – and have often been amused that our students didn't realise we don't hang ourselves up in the cupboard at three o'clock on Friday afternoon...

Teaching tip

There's such a thing as too much personal information; school staff have a right to privacy and an out-of-school life. We're not suggesting sharing personal emails or phone numbers, even though we're advocating partnerships with parents; these are professional partnerships.

Taking it further

In relation to pets, why not have a section on the website with pictures of staff with their pets, and which parents and families can add to with their own photos?

This idea suggests letting families know more about school staff, to help build those important relationships.

- As far as possible, have photos of relevant staff on the website – 'relevant' means staff that parents are likely to encounter, so includes reception staff as well as teaching staff.
- Schools, particularly secondaries, are confusing places. Have a map on the website, clearly labelled. Have copies available for any time parents are likely to come into school.
- Include photos and biographies of governors as well as teaching staff.
- Include information that staff are happy to share, as well as just names: Mrs Jones is a keen sportswoman, about to run her third marathon! Mr Jones and family act as short-term carers for animals from the local shelter.
- Think about the titles used for staff: don't just say that someone is the 'SEN coordinator' or 'literacy lead', as that may not mean much to parents. Explain what these members of staff do and how it impacts on young people.
- Remember that commonalities create a sense of connection. The more that parents feel they have something (anything!) in common with you, the more likely they are to feel able to have conversations with you about the important stuff (their child's learning and progress at school).

Handbook for Year 7 families

'They tell us about what they will be learning, but I am more interested in what [my child] will be eating and the school's mobile phone policy.'

Transitions are difficult times, not just for students but also for families. You'll already have materials to support the process of transition, such as a handbook for students and families or information on the school website.

But are you including the information that parents and families really need? And how will you know? One school found a simple solution: they asked Year 8 parents what they wished they'd known at the start of Year 7. That information was integrated into the handbook by the parents themselves!

- At transition days, ask incoming parents and young people what they really want to know.
- Ask Year 8 students and parents what they wish they had known.
- Never underplay the importance of knowing what something will look like. Incorporate photos of the school buildings, classrooms and staff... and don't forget reception staff, as they are likely to be among the members of staff parents interact with most often!
- If the school phone number leads to a series of options, consider including the list in the handbook; again, it's all about removing anxiety, and if a parent is phoning the school, knowing what number to press quickly can help.
- Make sure that the handbook is created in a way that reflects the parents' journey – perhaps sections on the 'first week', 'how children can excel', 'topics they will cover in the first term' and 'how you can boost their learning at home'.

Teaching tip

We know you know but it bears repeating: check with staff before sharing any photos or information.

Taking it further

Consider adding a 'How can we improve this handbook?' section to whatever you use for parents at transition so that you can keep updating it.

Bonus idea ★

Keeping good records will save you time in the end: keep a copy of every handbook each year, along with suggestions about making it better and what's been done to improve it from year to year.

Supporting family learning

'It takes a village to raise a child.'

Before we suggest ideas for how parents can practically support their children's learning at home, it is important that schools understand the nature of family life in 2020.

Taking it further

The proverb at the start of this idea mentions a 'village'. It's worth remembering that teenagers often interact with a lot of different adults, so having a sports coach, for example, at parents' evening may smooth the way to some conversations.

Many young people will return home from school to an empty house (so-called 'latchkey kids'); they will often prepare meals for themselves and manage their own time. Some may even be caring for younger siblings who return home before parents or carers do. In many households, both parents work and hold down several jobs, sometimes where one parent works nights and requires a quiet household during the day. Family relationships and dynamics can be diverse; for example, where parents are separated or divorced, children may split their time across different households, each of which has a different set of rules and family timetable. Schools need to recognise these wider patterns in family structures and understand as far as possible the family typologies in their school communities.

- Let parents know that you are interested in supporting them to support their child, and that this necessitates understanding more about family life.
- Keep it simple. For example, rather than sending home a document that goes into great detail about what students will cover that term in physics, you might choose to text parents (who have opted in) a few days before a classroom test, to remind them when the test is and what it will cover. Simply ask parents to nudge their child to look over material on page 5 of their textbook (for example) and encourage them to take the test seriously.

- Most parents are very interested in their child's progress and don't appreciate waiting until they receive a school report, a term in, to find out how their child is progressing – or not. You might choose to have a blog that parents can access, where you talk in general terms about how students in that particular class did in the test. What did they do well? What else do they need to work on and how can parents help with that?
- Some students may struggle academically and their parents may require even more of your support and understanding. Again, simple ideas can go a long way. Phoning up and leaving voicemails (perhaps five a day to five different families?) about any 'green shoots' that you have observed will always be welcome and help to build up that all important parent–teacher rapport. Such positive praise also helps to nudge parents to have encouraging conversations with their children about their learning and school more generally.

Bonus idea

Do keep a record of which families you have contacted; this will not only save you time (in figuring out who has not had such contact), but will also ensure that you don't neglect those students who never cause issues – they need praise too!

Not every child is in a family

'The word "family" conjures up a particular image that will be different for everyone. Is it the right word to even use? I'm not sure.' (Secondary headteacher)

If you've read the previous ideas, you'll know we make the point that 'parent' is a catch-all term, and what we mean by it is 'any adult with a caring responsibility for the child or young person'.

Most young people you interact with are in a family – but, as of 2016, over 70,000 children were involved with the care system. That's a lot of young people and it's important to be aware of them and their experiences.

In a secondary school, where many people deal with each student, it can be confusing to keep up with who is responsible for what; this is even more the case with care-experienced young people. It's vital to ensure that young people in the care system or those who have been in the past, get all the support they can from school staff as well as other carers.

- Try to remember and be sensitive to the fact that not all young people are in families. Be careful about saying 'Take this home to mum' (a phrase that already contains an assumption about gendered division of labour in homes) or 'in your family...'.
- Make sure as far as possible that school records are kept up to date, including records for those in care.
- It can be difficult to connect with all the different agencies supporting young people, and to do cross-agency work – everyone has different forms and databases and keeps different information. We'd suggest you concentrate on the young person's *learning*.
- Don't neglect praising care-experienced young people, and let the relevant adult know that they are doing well.

Parents are teenagers who grew up

'They assume what works for some parents will work for all – why?'

Anyone who has raised more than one child – or taught more than one young person – knows that what works perfectly well for one may not work at all for another; this can be frustrating, but it's also a bit of the creative part of teaching.

As a professional, you have become – or are becoming – expert in adapting your teaching to a range of students, knowing what different individuals need and how to approach their differing learning needs. Our point in this idea is quite similar: parents need the same kind of personalised approach. After all, they're just students – individual students, with their own particular ways of learning and understanding – who have grown up. And in fact, the process of growing up generally means that they have even more different experiences and understanding to bring to bear on their learning.

Yet time and again, we've noticed that all parents – in a school or in a year group – are treated in the same way. And, of course, there are times when this is necessary, simply due to the number of families. But there are other times when it can be important to understand the difference among and between families.

- It can be important to understand cultural and religious differences among families – when do they celebrate feasts and holidays?
- Just as you didn't give up teaching when a class session or idea didn't work, don't give up on parents – or individual parents – when something doesn't go the way you expected it to. Instead, think about why, and what you can do differently next time.

Taking it further

One way of understanding familial differences is to think about how you found out that different families do things differently. Use this as a discussion starter in a session about supporting families. What was your first instance of seeing people do things differently? (This can be quite entertaining!)

Who are your parents?

'Partnership with parents? These teachers don't even know who we are.'

Any partnership begins with really getting to know each other. How can a school even begin to develop ways of building an effective partnership with its families without understanding as much about them as possible?

One difference between secondary and primary schools is the simple number of parents you deal with; we're not expecting you to know all of your parents in the same way. But it will go a long way towards setting up the type of relationships that will benefit young people's learning if you make the effort to show parents that you *want* to know them, both as individuals themselves and as they relate to their children.

- Keep it simple. At the point of transition, ask your parents about their families via a survey. Tell them why you want to capture that data: you want to ensure that you are working as far as possible in alignment with them. You can also tailor-make initiatives that reflect your parental community and are sensitive to cultural needs and expectations.
- Almost 17 per cent of adults in England can be described as having 'very poor literacy' – that will almost certainly include some of the parents in your school, so bear this in mind.
- Be aware of **all** parents, including those whose first language is not English and who may not have been through the same education system: don't assume that everyone understands how the system works.
- Parents are people in their own right as well as being parents: as far as possible, address parents as Mr/Ms/Mrs/Dr [surname], rather than someone's mum or dad.

Planning for parents

'They don't come – they never come, no matter what we put on.'

This lament is all too well known among teachers: no matter what efforts are made to support parents, they either don't take advantage of the events or it's only the same few – who could be described as 'the worried well' – who come along, and never the ones you really want to reach.

The situation is understandably frustrating – you put a lot of effort into something for parents, and they just don't bother turning up. In fact, this has been called a 'vicious circle': teachers put things on; parents don't come; teachers stop wanting to put things on. But there's a missing element in that circle: the research shows that it's more like 'teachers put things on for parents *that parents don't want to come to*, parents don't come...'

There are some important questions to consider before even beginning to plan events for parents:

- Is it something that parents want?
- Is it at a time when they can come to the event?
- Is it in a place that they can get to and get home from at the time at which it's offered?
- What has been done in the past around this subject, and how successful was it? What can you learn from past events?

> **Bonus idea** ★
>
> Make sure that you have up-to-date transport timetables that relate to all of your families. Keep these up to date, and keep them somewhere that's easy to access. Also consider simplifying them, if at all possible (London bus timetables have been used as tests of numeracy, due to their complexity!). Make this information available for parents – perhaps on the website, on a page called 'How to get to us'.

Watch your language

'Words carry assumptions and assumptions create stereotypes, which are never helpful.'

Language is important and so are the terms that we use to describe people. Many of us, for example, may have grown up with a nickname that we disliked, or might react badly to having our names mispronounced or being wrongly addressed – all quite understandable.

Taking it further

What terms could you use to replace 'hard to reach'? You need terms that show that communication is a two-way street, so that both sides – parents and school – have to be involved. This might be part of a brainstorm at a staff meeting or governing body meeting, and something to work on with NQTs, for example.

Moreover, the language that we use demonstrates underlying assumptions and understandings. Many terms are now no longer used because of their racist or misogynistic meanings, to provide another example.

The same is true of the language that we use to describe parents. Consider the term 'hard to reach': it immediately sets up parents as being the issue; the *parents* are hard to reach when, in reality, parents have often reported that they find schools difficult to reach (and to understand, even if they can reach them!). The term puts the blame on the parents for being unreachable.

There are a lot of phrases that get called into use in relation to parents that are judgemental or negative, and proceed from a deficit standpoint. Phrases include examples such as 'hard to reach', 'that kind of parent' and even 'poor parent' – does that refer to a parent facing financial challenge or a parent not doing a good job (in the speaker's opinion) of raising a child?

Changing the language that we use is an iterative process: it shows a change in mindset and, *at the same time*, helps that change along. In that spirit, we'd like to suggest some other changes:

- Stop using the term 'hard to reach' for individual parents or groups of parents. The term puts the blame for problems in communication at the parents' door, and while that may be the case sometimes, our work and research has shown that the problems are often more evenly distributed. Throughout the rest of this book, you'll find suggestions for ways in which to communicate more frequently, and to better effect, with a wide range of parents.
- The same is true about phrases such as 'What can you expect from parents like that?' What you can expect is that parents love their children and want the very best for them. Start from there, because that's the point that you have in common with parents, rather than starting from the problematic areas.
- Think about the reasons why parents might be considered to be 'hard to reach'. What are the barriers that get in the way of communication and dialogue? How can these barriers be overcome? How can you meet parents halfway?

Bonus idea	★

If you're starting a book or journal club, as suggested in Idea 19, you might consider reading around issues such as critical race theory, which will help you think about uses of language.

Find out what parents want

'Parents love to be asked, that's for sure. I think it makes them feel valued.' (Headteacher)

As mentioned in Idea 43: Planning for parents, you're far better off putting on events (or bringing in new software) if you know that it's something that parents want, and can and will use or attend.

Teaching tip

Consider titles carefully. One school we know couldn't get parents to come to sessions on 'Teenage behaviour problems'. When they changed the title to 'I've got a teenager, get me out of here!' the take-up was much better!

It's also important to find this out from as many parents as you can – not just those few that you know well and who come to everything. They're not the ones who really need your support, after all (although they are still important).

This means that you need good, reliable means of communication with your parents. And it's important, for many groups of parents, that 'communication' is a plural noun – one method of communication is not going to be adequate for most parental bodies, and you may need more than one. These could include:

- Put suggestion boxes in places where parents are likely to frequent, with paper and pens handy (have them out at parents' evenings).
- Create a 'suggestions' email – something like 'suggestions@ourschool.co.uk'. Make it easy to remember and use, and make sure that it is monitored regularly.
- Hang large sheets of paper in places where parents are likely to be, again with pens handy. Let parents write suggestions on the pages or on sticky notes that are then stuck to the paper. (It's a good idea to take a photo of the sheets before moving them – this not only provides a record but also covers you in case something happens to the sheets in transit!)

Bonus idea ★

See Idea 67 about the importance of closing the feedback loop. Let parents know what you've done on the basis of their suggestions.

Setting up to support – an iterative process

Part 5

ROIDH – records or it didn't happen

'I couldn't understand it until I saw the diagram – then it all made sense!'

Our title for this section is based on the internet abbreviation POIDH: 'pictures or it didn't happen'. We're not saying that if you don't keep good records of your work around supporting parental engagement, that work didn't happen – but we are saying that if you do keep those records, it will be much easier to learn from what worked, to not repeat what didn't and to figure out why it didn't work.

We've already acknowledged that teachers are short of time (as are parents!). In this idea, we're making suggestions that should help to save you time in the long run.

When you prepare for a new year's teaching, how often do you go back to what you've done before? One of the things that most teachers learn early on in their careers is the importance of keeping materials from one year to another, and keeping those materials in a way that makes it easy to find what you want, when you want it.

The same ideas apply to supporting parental engagement. We've found in working with schools that often there is no record of what happened in previous years, and even if there is a basic record, there isn't a repository of invitations, email templates or evaluations. This means that everything has to be created from scratch, every time – and *that* means that a lot of time is spent doing things that have already been done.

- Particularly in secondary schools, where there are generally a lot more staff and more formal divisions (such as subject departments or faculties), it's important that the materials and evaluations are available to everyone. Even if a template for an invitation to an event has 'The English Department' in bold letters, it's easier to change that to a different department than to create the invitation from scratch.

- Talk as a school about where these materials will be kept electronically (it's far more use to be able to download and update a Word document than it is to start copying from a piece of paper – this also saves paper and space).

- It's also important to keep records, not only of the materials that have been used (parental support sheets for different topics, for instance), but also of individual events for parents.

- As a basic minimum, we'd suggest recording:

  - title of the event
  - date and duration (for example, was it a one-off or a three-week course?)
  - target audience (all parents, all parents of Year 11 students, all parents of young people preparing for options...)
  - aim or objective: you're used to these; they're part of most lesson plans. Treat events for parents in exactly the same way: what do you want to achieve, and how will you know whether it's been achieved? What's the change you want to see through this event?

There is an event-planning template and an event-recording template available in the online resources for this book.

Did it work?

'Insanity is doing the same thing over and over again but expecting different results.' (Attributed to Albert Einstein)

Schools are — or have become — remarkably data-rich environments; it seems that every detail of school life is recorded somehow or other, somewhere or other.

However, evaluating this data, at least in our experience, tends to break down almost completely when it comes to work with parents. Often, when we ask whether schools have evaluated their work with parents, we're told that 'of course they have'. However, that evaluation is at the level of what is known in the trade as a 'happy sheet' — an 'evaluation' form filled in at the time of the event, which gives a very surface-level response to what has happened. While those sheets are helpful in relation to short-term issues, such as whether the venue was too hot or too cold, they're not helpful in letting you know the *impact* of the event, workshop or whatever it is you're evaluating.

The kind of evaluation that is really useful should take place not just once, but over a period of time. If you've ever attended training run by one of us, the chances are high that you've been asked to put a note in your diary for a few months after the training, to remind yourself to reflect on the day and what you've done as a result of it.

To be helpful, evaluation needs to take place over a longer period, and to be far more in-depth than a sheet that simply says 'I enjoyed the evening'.

- Make evaluation a central part of your record-keeping system — get into the habit of writing and recording short evaluations as a matter of course.

- Plan evaluation as you plan your events – work evaluation into the processes.
- Ask people to record what they've learned and what they are going to do differently as a result of the event.
- Collect these ideas and publish them (anonymously) in a way that will be seen by most of your parents – for example, on the school website, on social media and in the school foyer.
- What you really want to know is not whether or not people enjoyed a particular event, but whether or not that event has had an impact that can't necessarily be seen on the day.
- Celebrate what has been learned and what's changing.
- Make it easy for parents and colleagues to give you evaluations: email them simple forms or questions, or use something like Google Forms (the simpler you make them, the easier it is to get the information from them!).

Bonus idea ★

One way of evaluating things is to ask people to write letters to themselves about what they will do differently, and then mail those out after a certain period of time – a few weeks or months, depending on what is appropriate.

Getting governors on board

'Why would you leave out the very people we rely on to shape the direction of the school? We invite them to everything.' (Headteacher)

In our work with schools, we rarely encounter governors as part of a team working with parents, and we don't understand this omission.

Try to have support for parental engagement with learning as a standing item at governing body meetings, just as it should be at staff meetings.

School governing bodies are often not representative of their parent groups; rather, school governors tend to be drawn from the group of parents who are comfortable coming into school and working in the way in which schools work. As your relationships with parents improve, consider asking those who are not already involved with the formal side of the school to join the governing body.

Governors in state-maintained schools in England and Wales have overall responsibility for the strategic direction and planning in the school. It seems obvious, therefore, that they should be involved in discussions and planning for parental engagement in learning, as it can have such an important impact on young people's outcomes. Moreover, governors will have to answer questions from inspectors about the planning and outcomes in the school, including work with parents.

- Invite all governors to any staff training around parental engagement. If governors can't come to such training, try to make sure that the materials are available to them and that someone reports on the training – and its outcomes – to a full governing body meeting.
- Just as you should ensure that all staff understand what effective parental engagement is, make sure that your governors also understand this.
- Parents often have little idea what the governing body does (if they know it exists at all). It's useful to have a dedicated section of the website for governors, and to highlight governors – and their work – in places that parents will see (such as on the website or in the foyer at parents' evening). Ask governors to be in attendance at times when parents will be in the school, and to introduce themselves informally.

In the community or part of the community?

'At the SLT training, they wanted us to talk about how we work with local communities, but they didn't actually invite any community leaders to the day.'

You may think you have more than enough on your plate just covering aspects of the seemingly ever-changing curriculum. But you know that your students exist outside of the classroom and so do their families.

The young people in your school are already part of wider communities (note the plural – they may be part of a religious community or one built around a sport or other activity, as well as the local geographic community). The same holds for their parents, who are likely to have even wider networks, through work, extended families, friendships and other groups. Your school exists in a community, but is it *part of* the community?

- Pool the knowledge that staff have about the community: whose opinion counts? Who are the movers and shakers in the community?
- Once you've figured that out, consider how you can connect with them. Could they be invited into school to give a talk? Maybe they could give a talk for parents.
- Perhaps there is a case for someone from the school going out and visiting various community groups to make those links.
- If staff are willing, you could create a network map showing all the connections that staff already have in the community – sports teams, choirs, and so on.
- Do you invite local business leaders to key school events? Many local businesses want to show that they support education and may even be happy to sponsor school fetes!

Opening the school gates

'They've got a welcome mat in the school. It's false advertising, though – no one's welcome there!'

We would like to think that the days of signs saying 'No parents past this point' are long gone (although we suspect that they are not, and certainly such signs existed in recent memory).

The sign itself – as is so often the case – means more than the simple words. It means that the school – and the learning that takes place in it – are the purview only of school staff (and the students), with parents and others playing no part in that learning.

First off, that's demonstrably false: many, many years of research and practice have shown the importance of families in young people's learning. Secondly, it's remarkably presumptive and arrogant. It's saying, 'We know all about learning' (and if that's the case, why are you reading this book?). No one knows 'all about learning' – we're all still learning about learning, every day and all the time and, more importantly, 'No one else knows anything about it.'

- 'Opening the school gates' isn't just a matter of physically opening the gates; it can be about explaining the gates – and the system to get through them – to all parties.
- As we've said elsewhere, having photos of what the school looks like – inside and outside – helps to remove some of the anxiety that parents and others might feel about visiting the school.
- The website can be an effective barrier to communication with the school, as can the way in which communications from the school are couched.

> **Bonus idea** ★
>
> Saying 'No parents past this point' is not the same as saying 'No pushchairs past this point, please' – we've known schools where this was a simple requirement due to the narrowness of the corridors. If this is the case in your school, have you thought about providing a place where parents could leave pushchairs and prams if they can carry their little ones on into school?

What does your website say about you?

'I never look at the website – what's the point? It still has pictures and information up there from last year!' (Parent)

Websites are the shop window for any school. Parents will absorb the images, read the wording and make decisions about what kind of school it is: its ethos, values and approaches to learning.

Ideally, any school website would have a section for parents that doesn't just pass on information about when the hockey matches and school trips are, but also shares information necessary to launch an effective home–school partnership. Sharing only administrative information with parents sets the tone that their job is simply to get their children to places on time and pack their lunches; it doesn't convey a message that if students are truly to thrive, we must work together, in an effective and respectful partnership. Some ideas for conveying this may be:

- Share a few quotations that convey the power that parents have to improve children's ability to thrive at school, derived from the parental engagement literature.
- Convey the difference between parental involvement and parental engagement in learning (perhaps through images).
- Acknowledge where and how you welcome parental support.
- Include video clips of a current parent talking to a teacher about what that partnership looks like and 'whose job it is to do what'.
- Provide a space where parents can submit comments about anything they are worried about relating to their child's learning. After answering individual queries, you could create a useful FAQ section.

Teaching tip

Websites for secondary schools typically do not show staff profiles with associated qualifications and images. We think that this is short-sighted, as parents need to be able to see 'who is who' at school.

Bonus idea ★

Parents are more likely to trust you and the school if they know a little bit about you: your qualifications, background and a little bit about why you joined the teaching profession. A little bit of self-disclosure can ease the parent–teacher relationship, even virtually!

IDEA 52

Making the most of the website

'The website? I never use it – I can't find anything on it and it's never updated; it's just confusing and useless!'

Building on the previous idea, remember that your website is the face that the school presents to the world; for many parents and students, it's the first introduction that they have to your school.

This is another case in which it's useful to work backwards from the effect you want to have. Ask yourself these questions:

- What's the overall aim of the website? Is it for staff? (If so, put it on the intranet, not the internet.) Is it for people interested in the school? Is it for current parents? Students? All of the above?
- What impression do you want to create in the minds of those who look at the website?

Some of the things that you *don't* want people to think are that the school is disorganised, sloppy or not up to date – all things that it's easy to think about a school when the website is poorly organised, when it doesn't clearly signpost where information can be found, or when the welcome letter is from the last headteacher but three...

It seems to us (and we look at a great many school websites) that some schools go for websites that are overly complex, difficult to understand and impossible to navigate.

- Remember that a lot of your parents may be accessing the website on a mobile phone or tablet; make sure that the website is optimised for being viewed that way.
- Signposting is at least as important as content – if parents (and others) can't *find*

information, they can't use it.

- Include a clear map of the layout of the school on the website, and ensure that the labels on rooms are the ones that are used in day-to-day conversation. (One of us spent 20 minutes lost in a school once because we'd been told to go to the Bunny Classroom – it was an infant school and every classroom had bunnies on it, but none of them had a label!)

- Think about the answers to the questions above – perhaps it's worth having clearly labelled sections of the website for different users?

- You need to use plain language when communicating with parents, and this applies even more so to your website – make sure that everything is easy to understand and navigate.

- Consider having a virtual tour of the school – either as a video (perhaps made by students as part of their coursework?) or as static photos. Seeing what the school will look like can relieve a lot of anxiety for new parents and students.

- Ask parents what they want to have on the website. Some suggestions might be:
  ○ a clear calendar that includes anything students might need to bring into school, in good time
  ○ an introduction to new members of staff
  ○ rotating biographies of members of staff – include non-teaching members of staff, and include information above and beyond academic information (obviously with the permission of the staff members involved).

Taking it further

Any pictures, photos or videos should have alternative text; make sure that the website is compliant with accessibility standards.

Pictures tell a thousand words

'Look at that! It shows a parent and child in a book-lined room... that bears no resemblance to the experience of the families in this school at all!'

One of the key images that we enjoy using to convey what great parent–school partnership looks like is that of a relay team, passing the baton to each other. No one likes to drop the baton! By working together and understanding each other's role in the partnership, we can make progress in supporting students.

The term 'parental engagement' can be meaningless to parents when plastered on the school website or mentioned in the school prospectus but not backed up by the way in which the school interacts with families. Images can more clearly convey the kind of partnership you are aspiring to have with parents.

- Consider the images that you use in key areas such as the reception and those that you use in your marketing material. Is there a non-threatening image of two adults talking positively and constructively?
- The difference between parental involvement and engagement comes to the fore here. Parents coming into school, attending events and baking cakes for the end-of-year fete is nice but won't drive academic outcomes. We are aiming for parental engagement in learning. Images that convey parents supporting their children at home (through dialogue, support and taking an interest) are powerful reminders that parents are able and *expected* to play a leading role.
- Make sure that any images you use of parents show a wide range of people in that role. Are there pictures of fathers or grandparents? Do the images reflect the make-up of your school in terms of diversity and family structures?

Bonus idea ★

Existing parents with whom you enjoy a positive partnership can help when it comes to providing quotations for the school website or magazine. In one school we worked with, the first chapter of the school prospectus was about shared values between parents and staff. It had positive images attached to it and would have made any parent feel welcome and, indeed, a valued partner.

Tracking communications

'The school only ever talks about "data, data, data"! Are there any people in that school?'

Think how long your partnerships at home would last if all you ever did was report to them, you never had a conversation with them and importantly, never listened to them.

Some of us are old enough to remember when school was about sitting still and listening to the teacher, taking down what they said and reporting that back in an exam. Teaching has moved on in leaps and bounds – we now understand the importance of interactions and personal relationships for learning. But unfortunately, many schools still seem to be stuck in the 'I talk, you listen' mode of working with parents. Parents' evenings are about reporting (not dialogue) and induction evenings are often simply about handing over information.

Most schools keep good records of how and when to contact parents. Within the appropriate confines of GDPR, these same lists can be used to contact parents on an ongoing basis. Keep a database of all communications with parents – for positive reasons (for example, to compliment a young person), as well as when issues arise. This needn't be onerous if the database is constructed in a thoughtful way.

We'd suggest that the database should record:

- every time a parent receives a positive communication and every time a parent is contacted about a problem
- communication over trips, permission slips, sporting events, parents' evenings
- communication about events aimed at parents and families
- responses to communications *from* parents – who responded, when and how?

Teaching tip

One advantage of tracking communications is that it makes it very simple to see who has (or has not!) been contacted.

Bonus idea ★

Suggest that every teacher – perhaps one department a term – contacts one parent a day to say something positive, and use this database to make sure that every parent receives good news at least once a term. The database should make it easy to keep track.

Policies in plain (language)

'I never understand anything that school sends home — it's all in teacher-speak; ordinary people can't understand that.'

Have you ever walked out of an appointment with a doctor or other professional and wondered what it was that you'd just been told?

That's actually a very common experience for parents whenever they deal with schools. We therefore want to talk about writing policies that can be understood without the need for an educational glossary. (We think it's indicative of the current state of schooling that, in teaching undergraduates about education, we have to provide a glossary of 'educational terms'.)

- Having policies — particularly any policies that will be shared outside the school — in language that everyone can understand will make life easier, not only in working with parents, but also in working with colleagues from other services (health, social services, police, and so on).
- We'd suggest dealing early on with the policies that most directly relate to parents and others outside of school: prioritise the behaviour policy (which parents will need to understand if there are discussions about poor behaviour), homework policy, uniform policy, and so on.
- However, we'd suggest that you *start* with the teaching and learning policy. Your teaching and learning policy needs to be clear for anyone affected by it: students, parents, families — everyone who cares about the teaching and learning in the school.
- Your governors can be your allies here: many of them will come from areas other than schooling, so ask them to read the policies and then ask them whether the policies are clear, and if not, why not?

> **Teaching tip**
>
> Make sure that all relevant policies (and we would argue that includes all policies that don't relate only to staff) are available and easy to find on the website.

Keeping track of it all in a large school

'We are so busy that we sometimes forget to keep a record of all the brilliant stuff that we do.'

Whichever ideas you are thinking of implementing from this book, keep a track of them. Work out what outcomes you are looking for and work backwards.

You may wish to see more parents coming in on parents' evening – great! How many? From which year groups? What will you therefore implement in terms of strategy that may help to drive this goal? How will you evaluate whether or not it has been a success? What might the barriers be and how can they be overcome?

Make sure that your targets are SMART:

- Make them **S**pecific: don't use 'increase parental engagement' but do use 'make sure that every parent in Year 7 has a positive phone call in term one'.
- Make them **M**easurable: record the number of calls, who is called and who called.
- Make them **A**ttributed: know who is supposed to make the call and who did.
- Make them **R**ealistic: don't make targets that no one can reach (such as every parent in the whole school gets a positive phone call in the first week); that sets people up to fail, means that nothing gets done and sours the whole process.
- Make them **T**ime-related: specify the timescale, for example, the first term, over the year.

Keeping track of the ideas that are implemented may require simple, cost-effective methods to capture change; see Idea 46 for some suggestions.

Teaching tip

We've suggested several times that some of the actions related to parental engagement should be part of targets: whole-school targets, personal targets, NQT targets, and so on. We're going to suggest it again here, but this time with the proviso that the targets are SMART (see left).

Get out of school

'How do I get them to come in?' (Headteacher)

Our response is usually: 'Why do you need them to come in? What's so special about this place that you can't meet parents somewhere else?'

It can be hard for teachers, who come to school every day, know it inside out and are comfortable there, to realise how intimidating schools can be for many adults. This is even more the case with parents who are new to secondary school: secondaries are often much larger, busier and more confusing than primary schools, and many adults are intimidated by the sheer number of people. We're not saying that you should never have meetings at school; rather, we're suggesting that you think about where else you *might* have meetings and why.

- Are there places in your catchment area where you could have meetings or hold workshops? Think about places that might work for formal workshops (perhaps the leisure centre rents rooms) or for just meeting a parent for coffee and a chat. How well do you know your area?
- Parents are another obvious resource for finding alternative venues: they are likely to know the area well.
- Consider barriers when you choose meeting places. Is there public transport (and is it still available when the event ends)? Do parents have safety concerns about visiting the venue or returning home in the dark?
- Try not to have all out-of-school events in just one place; parents in a large secondary school are likely to be widespread, so try to find places throughout the catchment area.
- Video chats could be another good idea, particularly if parents are spread across a large area.

Social media and phones in school

'Parents buy children phones but school policies set expectations around usage. We need to work together.' (Headteacher)

There is little doubt about it. The online world has an influence on children's behaviour, self-esteem and wellbeing levels. An appetite for social media can lead to less sleep, which can exacerbate feelings of anxiety and low mood.

Social media can also affect learning. This is why it is critical to share some evidence-based tips with your parents.

- Look at your school mobile phone policy. What does it actually say? Is it based on the available evidence?
- Don't send mixed messages. Some schools seem anti-phones but then insist that students have a phone for the journey to and from school.
- WhatsApp can be wonderful for connecting with one another. However, in schools, it can become a platform for gossip, cyber-bullying or the circulation of inappropriate messages. It is designed for people over the age of 16, so why not set the tone with parents in this regard? Many think of it as a simple, innocuous app, but it is how it is being used that matters.
- Also point out to parents that if they allow their children to access social media before the stated age, the app then thinks the children have turned 18 long before they have!

Social media is one area where we really need to seek alignment as far as possible between parents and schools. Transition is the perfect point in the school journey to ensure parents understand the benefits and risks of social media, the rationale behind age restrictions and the concept of 'digital hygiene'.

Teaching tip

Ensuring that children understand how to navigate the digital world safely needs all hands on deck, and schools can play an important role in shaping the discussion.

Taking it further

This is another area where it's very important for the school to share current research findings with parents. Don't be swayed by newspaper reports or Twitter discussions; go to the research! You could start with this open-access article: Lepkowska, D. (2019), 'To ban or not to ban? Mobile phone use in schools', *British Journal of School Nursing*, 14, (10), 510–11.

Bonus idea ★

Don't create a mobile phone policy for the school – CO-CREATE the policy with parents.

Vault (or at least surmount) the barriers

Part 6

(Re)building bridges

'You don't need to tell me about school – I remember school. All too well, I remember school – I hated every minute of it!'

Before you can really begin to overcome parents' barriers to engagement, you need to understand what those barriers are.

Taking it further

It's not really fair that you have to pick up the slack for the actions of those in the past who made parents fear or dislike school. So it's all the more important that we make sure that the next generation of teachers knows better! If you work with NQTs, make sure you discuss these ideas with them or with any early career teachers.

There are generally two main barriers that parents face when trying to engage with their children's learning and with schools. The first is time: parents are busy people. Teachers are also busy people, and several ideas in this book discuss saving time for everyone involved.

However, we want to mention the other barrier: parental experience of education and schooling. We often say to teachers that, in working with families, they are trying to rebuild bridges that others, before them, broke down (sometimes with extreme prejudice). It's important to understand that, while for many teachers and others working in schools schooling was an overall positive experience (we all had bad days, of course), for many parents there was precious little about their schooling that they can remember fondly.

- School may have been a place of being shamed: for their work, for their attendance (which sometimes was not within their ability to change) or for myriad other issues, including accent, language, dress, and so on.
- School may have been a place of constant failure.
- Remember that many parents may see you as a 'template teacher' and assume that all teachers are the same (and, to be fair, teachers often assume the same about parents). You need to find ways to show parents that you are not like the teachers who may have made them so unhappy in the past.

Beware when talking barriers

'I get confused – are we talking about parents working with us or with their kids?'

Think about Idea 59: (Re)building bridges, when you were asked to consider barriers to parental engagement. Is that really what you were thinking about? Or were you thinking about barriers to parental involvement with schools?

It's important to realise that parental engagement with learning and parental involvement with schools are not the same – and they may not have the same barriers. For example, none of these necessarily keep parents from engaging with their young people's learning:

- not coming into school
- not answering emails or texts
- not attending workshops, concerts and fetes
- not coming to parents' evenings.

Things that are far more likely to impede parents' engagement with learning include:

- parental lack of self-confidence in relation to learning
- parental experience of education (often leading to the above)
- parental lack of time
- parental lack of expertise, if they are being asked to help with content.

Often in our work with schools, and in the wider literature, we've found that school staff can blame parents for their lack of engagement, often without realising – see Idea 44 for more on this.

Bonus idea ★

Use part of the time in a staff or department meeting to list the barriers that staff think cause a lack of parental engagement. Then go back to the difference between engagement with *learning* and with *schooling* – and tackle the barriers that deal with learning!

Language barriers: part one

'I listen to what my child's teacher says. I speak English, have done all my life. I have no idea at all what she's talking about.'

In some of our presentations, we use a slide with the following, taken from various sites on the internet: 'There's a fine line between a numerator and a denominator – only a fraction of people will find this funny.' We can always tell where the maths teachers are in any audience, because they're the ones that find it funny.

Taking it further

As part of an INSET day or other meeting, read through a few documents and circle the terms that come across as jargon. What other way could they be explained? Is it necessary to use those particular terms (and if so, is there an explanation within the document)?

We also tend to point out that teachers in general speak their own language. Like almost every profession, teachers have their own jargon, their own language and their own way of using language. (We're right about this, you know – if you ask people who don't inhabit schools what 'assessment for learning' means, you'll get some very funny looks!)

Jargon can be useful for all kinds of reasons, and one is that it quite simply saves time. You can say 'Ofsted' and people know what you mean; you can say 'PSHE' and not have to explain it to your colleagues.

But jargon has another function, as well: it shows, quite clearly, who is 'in' and who is 'out' of a particular group. If you understand the jargon, you're a member of the group. If you don't, you aren't.

And being on the outside is problematic not only because of the way it makes us feel (like outsiders and not members of the 'in' group), but also because it means that information is not getting to the people who need it. (This is easy to demonstrate – think of a conversation you've had with a doctor or other medical person where they thought they were being very clear and you had no idea what they were talking about...)

- It can be very difficult to realise when you are using jargon, for the very simple fact that it's an important part of your everyday working life – everyone you come into contact with, most days, understands what you mean when you use it.
- However, parents – unless they are themselves involved in the schooling system – don't understand the jargon you're using.
- There are two ways out of this, and we're suggesting that you deny the dichotomy and go with *both* rather than choosing one.
- Option one: explain the jargon. Create a glossary of 'school-based terms' that you can share with parents and other interested parties (because those you work with in other areas – social workers, police, and so on – will all have their own jargon and often won't share yours...). There is an example glossary in the online resources for this book, which you can use as a starting point.
- One way of creating this glossary is simply to ask parents which terms they don't understand. It's probably best to do this anonymously, such as having a suggestion box or asking parents at a meeting to circle all the terms that they don't understand in a document and hand it in (without signing it). Or you could put up large sheets of paper and ask parents to write the words and terms they don't understand.
- Option two: stop using the jargon. This will be easier once you know what parents are seeing as jargon.
- It takes confidence to not use educational terms and instead communicate in a language understood by parents.

Bonus idea ★

When trying to identify jargon, try asking students which terms their parents ask them to explain.

IDEA 62

Careful of the cost

'I don't have the money to order things online like other mums.'

Just as schools are facing financial restrictions, more and more families are in poverty: the number of children in poverty in England is very high and still climbing.

Teaching tip

Have a look at the Poverty Proofing the School project (www. povertyproofing.co.uk) and see if any of the ideas there would be useful in your context.

The fastest-growing group of families in poverty are those families in which at least one adult member of the household works. And while schools in England (and elsewhere) are not supposed to charge for 'education provided during school hours', many events in schools amount to much the same thing. Consider how often you ask families for money that impacts on the school day over the course of a year. Some examples might include:

- Red Nose Day
- Yellow T-Shirt Day
- Odd Socks Day
- Children in Need.

These are not the only days that present a call on the family purse: also consider non-uniform days and World Book Day, among many other similar events. Days such as these benefit laudable charities, and it is, of course, a positive thing for children to know that these charities exist and to support them if they can. However, recent research has shown that even children in primary school are aware of financial pressures on their families and do what they can to mitigate these; looking at your attendance registers on the days mentioned above might be instructive.

Yes, most of these events 'only cost a few pounds' but, for some families, those 'few pounds' are simply too much — and that's the case for an increasing number of families, as school staff know only too well. Moreover, a lot of families move in and out of poverty, and some may not qualify for free school meals or additional support yet still face real financial struggles.

- Consider how you work around families facing economic challenges – don't have lists of young people in receipt of additional funding out in the open, for example.
- Also be careful of assumptions – at the start of the year, remember that, for some students, the summer has been difficult, to say the least. Statistically, many in your school will have been hungry and living in insecure accommodation. Don't assume that everyone went on holiday and don't ask young people to write about their summers – instead, it might be useful to ask them what they hope for the school year ahead.
- New uniforms can create a serious financial burden for families. If your school is thinking about changing its uniform, be sure to talk to families before any decisions are taken – and follow the guidelines about having various suppliers rather than one dedicated supplier of uniforms.

Taking it further

Google and share 'The Cost of a School Day Toolkit' from the Child Poverty Action Group with colleagues. How did it make you think differently? What might you want to change in school as a result?

World Book Day

'When you've spent six weeks knitting Hermione Granger's scarf, only to be told with a few weeks to go that it's going to be a Roald Dahl day, you want to weep...' (Emma Soares, mum)

We've given World Book Day (WBD) its own idea because it's become such a big thing in the last few years. Weeks before the day, supermarkets and other outlets are full of costumes for parents to buy for their young people.

Taking it further

If you have crafting clubs, perhaps they can help to create toys based on favourite children's books for local charities. Ask parents and other family members for ideas.

Although we realise that dressing up might be more of a primary-school-focused activity, we thought that we would use this opportunity to provide some ideas about how WBD can be celebrated even in secondary schools.

- Remember that the whole point of WBD is *enjoyment of reading* and, hopefully, increasing the enjoyment that people take in reading.
- WBD might also give staff an opportunity to showcase their love of reading to students and to discuss favourite authors, but also book genres that they do not enjoy.
- Remember that 'reading' doesn't have to be the canonical texts – while some of your students will certainly enjoy reading Dickens, others might well prefer Gaiman, Pratchett or Pullman.

There are many, many ways to celebrate WBD that are appropriate to secondary students (and staff!) and have nothing to do with dressing up.

- Ask everyone to put the name of their favourite book on a sticky note and place the notes on large sheets of paper in communal areas. Collate the answers every year (keep records!) and see what changes and what doesn't.

- You could make the above idea into a quiz by trying to figure out whose favourite book is whose!
- Share the book audit findings in one big assembly. What books are most popular within each year group? Which genre is most popular?
- Many schools have links with various authors – it's always worth a try! This is probably particularly effective with authors of young adult literature, and not only the most famous ones; if you are lucky enough to have an author visit your school, invite the parents along (and do check whether any of the parents qualify as authors!).
- Don't stop at authors – try contacting the people providing illustrations! This can include books that students enjoyed when they were much younger.
- Ask students to ask adults in their families what their favourite books were when they were this age.
- Ask students to ask older members of the family or community for a story from their youth, and turn it into a story to be shared.
- Consider WBD as an opportunity for your school pupils to interact with younger pupils (perhaps in the feeder primary school). Maybe they can visit and read to younger pupils (great for the reader's self-esteem and nice to give back!) or donate time to struggling readers?

> **Bonus idea** ★
>
> Be creative and take the advice of creative colleagues. Just because WBD relates to reading, that doesn't mean that it has to be led by the English department – let the art department lead an illustration session for both parents and students!

Language barriers: part two

'Yes, but you can't say that in English!' (One of us, attempting to explain the concept of 'simpatico'...)

When we mention 'language barriers', you're probably thinking about those who speak languages other than English.

Taking it further

You could ask parents to translate key documents into particular languages for other parents in the school community.

There's a sort of odd bifurcation in British education: on the one hand, we constantly lament the low levels of students and teachers who are able to speak more than one language (we lag far behind most other European nations in this). We laud those who learn other languages. On the other hand, when we think about children who do speak more than one language, we often see that as a problem rather than a strength.

It seems to be another area where the system automatically sees 'deficit' when in fact it could quite easily see 'benefit'. There are, for instance, things that one can easily say in some languages that simply aren't possible in English. For example, the concept of *whānau* is used in some New Zealand documents; it's a Maori word that means 'family', but much more – extended family and links with others. It's almost untranslatable and so the word itself is used.

- Find out what languages your parents and families speak.
- Celebrate those languages! Create signs for the school in some of the languages, asking parents to help you.
- Ask parents whether there are words that might be useful for you to learn and use in and around school.
- Ask parents whether there are words that they need you to translate or differentiate. For example, a Polish colleague alerted us to the fact that 'home' and 'house' are not distinguished in her language, yet in English these can mean very different things.

Bonus idea ★

Remember that not all languages are verbal. If you have family members who use BSL or Makaton, for instance, you could work with them so that members of the school community learn appropriate and useful signs.

Summer needn't mean no learning

'As a child, I remember not being able to hold a pen properly after the summer holidays. We are trying to avoid that here.'

While students may not continue learning new *content* over the summer, they can continue *learning* and thinking about learning.

There are a number of things you can do to help this process along:

- Help parents to understand the value of doing a bit of schoolwork over the summer.
- Give parents and students at least an option for completing work online over the summer months. Give them a summer reading list and perhaps even one for parents (of books that staff have enjoyed in their leisure time).
- When communicating the importance of learning upkeep over the holidays, watch your tone. Parents are sensitive to the pressures that their children are under. Instead, try to frame the message along the lines of: 'Pace is important. By doing a little bit of work over the summer, the autumn term will feel less pressured and hopefully more enjoyable.' Parents understandably don't like the idea that lots of learning benefits might be lost over the summer because their children don't pick up a pen for its duration, so many will be receptive to the idea that their children do a little bit, while still finding time for lots of relaxation.
- Basically, the message is: what could our students be reading or doing over the summer that is fun, takes up little time and will help them to hit the ground running in September? Can we engage parental support for this idea?

Teaching tip

Another of the phrases that we'd like you to bin is: 'If they're not in school, they're not learning.' Rather, try thinking: 'What can they learn in the summer? How can we help families to encourage learning?'

Taking it further

Set expectations that any homework won't be marked over the summer months (you need your holiday), but perhaps the school might celebrate the work that students have kept up with on return to school in September.

Giving information vs dialogue

'We're really good at communicating with parents – we send stuff home all the time! It's not our fault if they never read it.'

Teaching is rarely about just standing at the front and giving information. It's about communicating with young people; it's about dialogue; it's about give and take.

Teaching tip

Have a good look at what goes home and see how much of it is related to learning. If things are constantly going home that aren't about learning, it's no wonder parents turn off and aren't interested.

In working with school staff around the issue of communication, we often ask people to consider how their romantic relationship would fare if all they ever did with their partner was exchange factual information: 'I taught this many sessions today.' 'We need two pints of milk.' 'The cat has a vet appointment at four o'clock.' Generally, the response is that the relationship would falter within a month, if not a lot sooner. That's because we all know that there's a difference between sending information and communicating; there's a difference between a hand-out and communication.

The same is true with parents and communication. Parents have told us that they carefully file all the information that comes home from school at the start of the school year, but that by Christmas, they are skimming things to find out whether there's anything they need to do, sign or give money to, or whether there is an issue around their child.

In terms of supporting learning – as you know, as a teacher – communication and dialogue are far more important than giving information. Communication and dialogue – often *about* information – are the elements that make learning solidify.

- Gather all the things that go home for an average student over the course of a month – paper-based, electronic, texts, messages, and so on.
- Is there some other way in which some of that information could be given to parents, if they need it? Could it sit on a website that they can easily access? (Don't assume the answer to this – ask parents!)
- When you do send things home or put them out, is there an easy way for parents to reply to you? Is that clear in the communication?
- Is it immediately clear which things are for noting (such as timetables and schedules) and which are for consultation (considerations of a new uniform, perhaps)?
- See Idea 67 about feeding back to parents and closing the feedback loop.
- Think about the immediate messages that the school sends out – on the webpage, in the reception, on the answerphone, and so on. Make it as easy as possible for parents and others to get through to you.
- Let parents know reasonable timescales for responses: one of the problems about email is that it can set up unrealistic expectations about responses. Let parents know (somewhere prominent) that 'We will respond to all emails within two working days' and then stick to it.

Taking it further

Bear in mind that a response doesn't have to be a complete solution – if it will take more than a couple of days to answer a query or find a solution to an issue, get back to the parent so that they know their message has been received, and tell them what steps you are taking in relation to their concern or issue.

You said, we did

'When parents realise that we take their feedback and do something with it, they are amazed.'

Many of us have had the experience of being told off (or doing the telling off) for not doing something that, in reality, we had already accomplished.

Teaching tip

This is another place where the skills you already have as a teacher can come in handy. You are practised at supporting learners, and showing young people where they have done brilliantly, as well as where they have made mistakes. You know how to use effective praise!

In our experience, schools are often in this situation. Parents tell us that 'The school never listens to what we say!' while, at the same time, school staff are telling us how they have acted on parents' suggestions. It's not that the school isn't doing what parents have asked them to do – it's that schools are not *showing* parents that their suggestions have been taken on board. (No one expects you to act on all parents' suggestions, as there will always be some, for example, who want more and some who want less homework...).

- Wherever you have a suggestion box or whenever you solicit ideas from parents, have some way of displaying what you've done on the basis of suggestions received in the past: 'Parents suggested that we put tips for parents on the website for each subject. You'll find them here!' (with a hyperlink).
- Be clear about what is, and what is not, up for negotiation. There are some things that you can't change, such as holidays or exam schedules. There are other things that you as a school may decide are not open for negotiation, and that's also fine – just be clear.
- Also be clear when consultations close or when suggestions on a subject are no longer being taken: 'Thank you for all of your suggestions about our new uniform; we're working through these now!' When you publicise the new uniform (or whatever it is), thank parents for their input.

Having difficult conversations

'This conversation is not going to go well... I know exactly how it's going to go and it's going to be bad for everyone.'

There's no getting around the fact that, at some point, you're going to have to have a 'difficult conversation' with a parent.

The conversation may be difficult because of a student's academic results, behaviour or a combination of the two. You may have to relay bad news of an exclusion or other consequences. We all know that it can get easier with experience, but it's never really easy.

- Consider taking advice from a colleague you trust, someone who seems to be able to deal with these conversations in a way that works well for everyone (not just for the teaching staff), particularly if this is one of the first 'difficult conversations' you've had.
- Remember that no matter how difficult it is for you to *tell* a parent news like this, it's far more difficult for the parent to *hear* news like this.
- Many parents – and we are no different here – feel defensive for their child. Know this going into the conversation, be prepared for it and don't react to it immediately.
- Keep good records of all conversations, and if there are things that need to be done or acknowledged, it might be worth following up with an email. If so, tell the parent why and emphasise that it's so everyone, including school staff, is clear about what's going on or going to happen.
- If possible, try to find a positive or look to the future: 'When she comes back after the day's exclusion, I think it would be good to...'
- The title of this idea is important: this should be a **conversation** and not a monologue. You need to give the parent information, but you also need to listen.

Helping parents to help

Part 7

How was your day?

'No, of course I don't answer her – but if she's not home, I go find her, make her ask and then I ignore her. But if she asks, I know she cares.' (A teenager, about her mother asking 'How was your day?')

Parents of secondary-age students often give up asking 'How was your day?' because the only answer they get is a grunt or a dull 'OK'.

Our own children apparently did very little in school – at least, that's what they said, as 'Nothing' was the stock reply to being asked what they did that day. However, young people themselves have told us that the question is still important. They made the simple link: if someone asks, then someone cares.

School (not to mention after-school activities) is tiring. Suggest to parents that bombarding their child with questions the moment they get in from school is not the best idea. Let them settle a bit and then have a discussion.

What's important isn't so much knowing precisely what students did each day, but rather *showing an interest* – let parents know that that's the important point. Also let parents know what we found in our research – keep asking the question (or a variant of it) because it lets the young person know someone cares.

You could also suggest some alternatives:

- 'Tell me two things you know now that you didn't know this morning.' (This can be a family activity, perhaps around the dinner table – parents can model that they are still learning!)
- Parents might ask their children to rate their day, say on a scale of 1 (horrible) to 10 (absolutely awesome).
- They might also ask young people about the best and worst bits of the day.

Bonus idea ★

For a form group or other pastoral activity, 'two things I've learned today' is a good starter – again, especially if the teacher joins in!

Worry not

'We have lots of anxious parents in our school and, as a result, lots of anxious students.' (Headteacher)

Anxiety is one of the most prevalent mental health disorders in older teens. It is on the rise too, especially in school-aged children, and girls are particularly affected.

Often schools are left to pick up on the early signs of mental distress, signpost to often-overstretched mental health services and do a lot of the one-to-one work required to support young people. However, there are a number of key messages and resources that should be passed on to parents of anxious children.

- Anxiety isn't always the enemy. Children of all ages need to get used to the feeling of having butterflies in their tummy, or a dry mouth before a presentation or a school concert, and learn to deal with it. Anxiety can enhance performance. Those same tummy butterflies can be truly positive feelings (associated with excitement, falling in love or positive expectation).
- Anxiety that inhibits a student from participating fully in activities that they normally enjoy is a red flag. Anxiety that prompts self-harming behaviours, stress, avoidance, emotional distress or panic needs to be taken very seriously and may require clinical attention.
- The good news is that there are lots of brilliant approaches that can really help young people to manage anxiety.
- Let parents know that soothing anxious students may not be as effective as *coaching them* to explore their worries, finding alternative ways of thinking that may reduce the anxious thoughts. When children recognise that their thoughts control their emotions, and by tackling thoughts they can improve their mood, they feel empowered.

Teaching tip

Parental mental health is highly correlated with children's, so be mindful of this as you work with anxious children and embark on supportive work with their parents.

Bonus idea ★

Recommend the book: *How to Talk to Your Child about their Fears and Worries* by Professor Cathy Creswell and Lucy Willetts to your parents. It was specifically written as a handbook for parents of anxious children and contains some excellent, evidence-based tips.

99

Share red flags early on

'We are on the frontline. We see the first signs of mental distress every day.' (Pastoral head)

Half of all diagnosable mental health disorders are diagnosed before the age of 14, but mental distress and the accompanying signs can be easily missed at secondary school.

Teaching tip

Plan for any difficult conversation with a parent. Ask a colleague if you can role-play what might happen. Put yourself in the place of the parent. Let the parent know what the chat will cover and give them a choice of how and where to have the chat. The main thing is that they are comfortable.

Schools need to be aware of what the red flags might be, and ensure that their staff understand these and are able to have conversations with parents about them. Bring parents' attention to potential red flags, such as:

- School refusal (which can be related to anxiety).
- Self-harming marks on arms. Do your staff know what to do next? Self-harming behaviours, particularly in boys, can be harder to spot.
- Negative language used by students to describe themselves. Phrases like 'I hate myself', 'No one likes me' or 'I am rubbish' may indicate low self-esteem or a need for more resilient thinking. Talk to parents about your concerns and share strategies with them that you use in school when you hear negative self-talk.
- Aggressive behaviour. This always demands careful exploration; it is an expression of frustration or disempowerment (perhaps at home) and may even indicate a child who is living with trauma, grief or toxic stress. Tread carefully and be compassionate.

Children with SEN often struggle with a range of challenges in schools that can be easily missed or dismissed as poor behaviour. Never be afraid to talk to parents about any behaviour that worries you. Showing that you care should be at the heart of any difficult conversations with parents and carers.

Supporting resilience

'Sometimes parents are afraid of letting children make mistakes. It is our job to normalise mistakes and help students learn from them.' (Headteacher)

Resilience is a prized trait. It is highly valued by schools, teachers and employers. We all want to teach, work alongside and even be in a relationship with people who are optimistic, flexible in their thinking and able to reframe life's challenges and bounce back.

There are three areas on which schools should help parents to focus when trying to cultivate resilience in students: emotional resilience, academic resilience and digital resilience. Schools can't affect what goes on at home but they can demonstrate how resilience can be cultivated through modelling, language and a focus on resilient habits. Consider the following areas to share with parents:

- How do you value resilience in students (what are you valuing in school reports, performance or effort)?
- How do you praise and motivate students? Can you share with parents what you do that you find really works?
- When students do bounce back from challenges, this needs to be recognised by both teachers and parents. 'Catch' resilience when you see it and share those lovely pieces of feedback with parents.
- Use consistent, positive language as a staff body when talking about resilience. Perhaps you have a metaphor that you can use or adopt as a school when referring to resilience (such as a coiled spring or a bouncing ball). Explain these images to parents.
- Talk to parents about digital resilience. Reiterate to parents the importance of having family discussions around what it means to 'bounce back' in the digital world.

Teaching tip

When conveying information to parents at parents' evening or in school reports, remember to value the fact that their child has made mistakes and learned from them. Point out how resilient their child is using concrete examples. Parents love to know that you have noticed and care.

Taking it further

Be sure that 'resilience' really is being resilient to legitimate pressures. Poverty, poor infrastructure and insecure housing are societal problems, and won't be solved by anyone being 'resilient'. You could discuss the difference and dividing lines as a staff group.

What do parents want to know? What do they need to know?

'If parents ask too many questions, we know we haven't given enough information. Simple as that.'

In our experience, parents want to know exactly what is expected of their child, whether in terms of what they need to bring to school each day or in terms of their academic work.

Parents can feel frustrated by a lack of timely information, and normally need time to absorb what can be a large volume of administrative information in advance of key events. Schools need to ease the administrative burden on parents. What do they need to know in advance and is the information conveyed in as easy a format as possible?

In terms of students' academic work, parents need to know on a short-term basis, in general terms, what their children will be studying – parents need enough information so they can discuss learning with their children.

- Have a ready-made reading list that parents can help their child to access over the half-term break. Genuine partnership in learning means working to build parental confidence as well as student confidence.
- Don't send all information to all parents. This is unnecessary and confusing – use the electronic means at your disposal (whatever is used by your school) to target information to the families and parents who need it.
- As we've mentioned, make it clear what parents need to *do* with the information you send – is it for noting? Acting on? If so, by when and who needs to know?

Bonus idea ★

You know that you broadly teach the same curriculum each year. This implies that you don't really need to constantly create new information sheets or resources for parents. When you are teaching the Battle of Hastings as a topic, for example, have ready-made questions or a quiz to send home to parents, so that they can check their children's knowledge.

Sleep matters

'Our students are not getting enough sleep but we are expected to deal with the implications of that in school. It is not right.'

The quality of sleep that young people are enjoying – or not – determines to a great extent how engaged and alert they will be in your classroom.

Recent research revealed that school-aged children in the UK are increasingly sleep-deprived. According to Health Behaviour in School-Aged Children – a survey about young people's wellbeing conducted in collaboration with the World Health Organization – over a quarter of young people are not getting enough sleep to feel awake and concentrate on school work. Clearly, sleep is a matter for family life and it's not your fault, nor is it your job to encourage teens to have an early night. However, when a lack of sleep impacts on learning, it can be an area of focus for schools.

Teaching tip

Schools often relish putting on workshops for parents around issues such as drug use or the perils of teenage drinking (both of which are actually on the decrease nationally) and forget to focus on the topic of sleep. Don't forget to include it!

- Try sharing information about how sleep impacts on learning and memory with students and parents.
- Encourage family research, where students might have to explore family sleep patterns and how they affect mood and productivity. One school science department used Fitbits to monitor quality of sleep against test scores. You can guess what they found...
- By engaging families in 'homework' like this, you can support parental engagement in learning and participative conversations between parent and child, and stimulate important family discussion.
- You will find that parents are very interested in the topic of sleep in general! It is a topic that provides a nice gateway to talk about other issues more closely related to learning.

Don't wait to support aspirations

'We set the tone, we start conversations, we nudge them towards things that might inspire them. For many of them, we are role models.' (Headteacher)

We know that parental expectations and aspirations for their children shape, to a great extent, students' desire and motivation to aim higher.

Teaching tip

We don't wish to suggest that every young person should go to university, but we do want to ensure that every young person who wants to go to university has a fair shot at doing so.

Understanding where we can head can help to motivate students to focus and study for their GCSE exams, for example. The earlier that schools can start a dialogue with parents and students about the range of options available to them, the better. The beginning of sixth form is far too late to start talking about universities.

- Help parents to understand that their goals and aspirations will shape those of their children.
- Consider putting on workshops and events that actually enable parental goals and aspirations. In doing so, you are helping parents to model ambition and strategies for reaching one's goals. For example, you might run a CV workshop for carers returning to work or a talk for those who wish to start a business.
- When helping parents to think about university as an option for their children, always acknowledge their worries, fears and any perceived obstacles first. For example, we know that many parents worry about their children getting into debt and may need reassurance as to how student loans work. Parents may worry about their children not getting a job after university, or being isolated and far from home. By understanding these worries, a school

is better placed to tackle any parental reluctance to university, which can be transferred to students.

- Model being proactive as a school. This means 'reaching out', asking for local businesses to facilitate student visits to their offices, and so on. We know of one secondary school that appealed on social media for a firm of architects who could show some aspiring young architects (from disadvantaged backgrounds) around their offices. Hey presto! This worked.
- Use your school network of alumni as a source of inspiration, talks and opportunities for students and parents. Many of them will be successful in their line of work and provide wonderful case studies of ex-students who have gone on to do exciting things.
- Seek out parents in your school community who have been to university (as first entrants from their families) and let them tell their story.
- Ask local businesses whether they will fund a particular school prize within a particular subject (for example, an engineering award for a young person who is excelling in design technology). Create opportunities for young people so that they can refer back to that experience in future applications.
- Some staff may wish to share their personal stories with parents (this may happen via a website page rather than a physical talk). In one school we worked in, a member of staff who had been raised in poverty shared her story with parents of how she became a teacher and eventual head of department. She shared who had helped her along the way and how they had shaped her thinking and impacted on her self-belief. You may even have a place on your website where individual journeys of this kind are celebrated and accessible to parents.

Taking it further

Read up on schemes such as 'Parent Power' at King's College London (which models ways of positively empowering parents to help their children reach university) or The Brilliant Club, which works with state schools via its Scholars, Researchers in School and National Tutoring Programmes.

'University's too expensive for us!'

'Why would I make my daughter do something that will get her into debt, when there is no guarantee of a job at the end of it?' (Parent)

It is perfectly understandable that parents worry about student finances and how their child will cope when they arrive into tertiary education settings.

It is therefore important to ensure that parents are aware from the start of secondary school that there are options beyond university; elite apprenticeships, work-based apprenticeships, colleges and graduate work schemes all offer a range of opportunities to young people that are aspirational and mean that young people can earn as they learn.

- Get financial information to parents at the start of Year 7 – waiting until A level is too late.
- Consider a subscription to Unifrog (www.unifrog.org), which shows all the available destination options to young people beyond secondary school in real time.
- Consider having a careers day in Year 7 or 8 so that young people can access ideas earlier rather than later. Always emphasise that they should follow their interests, passions and talents. Doing some preparatory work for these sorts of days can be beneficial.
- Don't have the career day just for students, though – include parents and families. It may not be possible to have them come in during the day, but some of the events could bleed over into the evenings.

Bonus idea ★

Create short podcasts (no more than five minutes) of some of the information about finances for university, and post these on the website (and make them easy to find!). You may need to do more than one to cover all the bases – just make the titles clear.

Don't neglect the usual suspects

'This school doesn't appreciate us. We're here all the time – we work in the library and all over the place, because we have the time to do it. But they never notice.' (Parent)

Just as in any relationship, it's all too easy to ignore the people who don't cause problems. But that doesn't mean that they are not just as important as those who do – it's just that they take up less of our time and energy.

A great deal of what is written about engaging parents focuses on those parents who are not perceived to be engaged – the ones covered by terms such as 'hard to reach', which we've already suggested you abandon. And that makes sense: the parents you find it difficult to communicate with may well take up more of your time than the parents you know you can rely on.

Most schools have a bank of such parents: they're your parent governors, they make up the PTA or parent forum, and they can always be relied on for concerts and fairs. But the 'usual suspects' also include students – those students you can always count on, who are on time, who are rarely absent, and who do good, steady work. You may not actually think much about them at all – they're just there when you need them.

- Ensure that the parents of the middle-band, steady students also know something good about their children from time to time.
- Don't neglect the parents that you count on. Remember the value of a simple thank you – send a card or a text, or highlight their work on the website.

Teaching tip

If you're trying to think about what you could say to a parent and you're a parent yourself, consider what you would like someone to say to you about your own child and go from there...

Not all bad all the time

'We never hear anything good from the school, except maybe at parents' evenings. Any other time they contact us, we know it's going to be bad news.'

Many of us have had the experience of working for or with someone who only ever got in touch when we'd done something wrong. You know the feeling – you see them bearing down on you in the corridor and you know what's coming. They say, 'Can I have a word?' and they mean, 'Let me tell you what you did wrong this time.'

For many parents, seeing the school's phone number pop up leads to precisely those sorts of feelings. Parents have told us that, by November, they are looking askance at anything that comes home from school to see whether: a) their child is in trouble, b) they need money or some other goods, or c) they need to sign something.

That doesn't sound to us like the basis for a good relationship, and it's certainly not the basis for a good partnership. While we may never get to the place where families greet every communication from the school with joy, there should at least be an even chance of the news being good in comparison to it being bad. And the only way to ensure that is to celebrate successes. You already know this – you know that a young person who receives praise as well as challenge is likely to be more comfortable in learning. Once again, parents are quite the same.

Celebrate everyone's successes:

- If your school has posted lists of 'Our students who got into Oxbridge' or 'Our students who got into university', consider perhaps replacing these or at least augmenting them with 'Our students who followed their dreams' – to be the best hairdresser or mechanic in the village, for example (after all, those are also vital parts of society).

- Take the time to praise students to parents. Don't wait for parents' evening, although don't neglect that, either – many parents have told us that they enjoy parents' evenings precisely because it's about the only affirmation they get that they are doing a good job as parents!
- Celebrate the successes of staff as well: if someone has finished an MA, for example, let parents (and other staff) know – after all, students are likely to benefit from such extended professional study.
- Don't limit celebrations to professional activities: if a member of staff has completed a marathon (particularly for charity), won an award or done anything else that you'd congratulate them about personally, ask them whether you can share it more widely!
- The same applies to parents and parent groups.
- Use the database suggested in Idea 46: ROIDH – records or it didn't happen to ensure that everyone gets a positive comment home at least once a term.

Managing maths and learned helplessness in families

'I'm no good at maths, so there's no way I can help my child with that! I just tell him to do the best he can and ask his teacher...'

Many secondary school parents struggle when their children have homework that involves maths; 2 + 2 is something that most of us can handle, but many people struggle from the point at which children encounter fractions.

Taking it further

We have created a video specifically on maths anxiety for parents, which you can share with them. The purpose of the video is to help parents reflect on their feelings about maths and how these might impact on their children's views. See the online resources for the link.

This is actually a very widespread feeling; many people have what has been called 'maths anxiety' – a feeling of panic, fear and inability to function when they encounter maths problems. Many parents also feel shame and guilt because they feel they are letting their children down by being unable to help.

We've included 'learned helplessness' in the title of this idea. Part of maths anxiety for many people is having learned to be helpless and think that they are 'not good' at maths. For many parents, this also means passing that fear and helplessness down to their children.

- Let parents know that it's not important to know the answers to questions that their children have about their maths work – in fact, it's probably best if parents *don't* try to help find the answers that young people should be finding for themselves.
- Let parents know that it's OK for them to say that they don't know the answer. They aren't failing their children; they are modelling the fact that they, too, are still learning.
- Parents and young people often have quite narrow views of 'maths'. It's worth pointing out the maths involved in figuring out points in football leagues, budgeting or saving for something, or working out how much paint will be needed for a DIY project.

Supporting parents of the digital generation

'Let's face it, they know more than we do. That scares me.' (Parent)

The parents you are currently working with are among the first generation to have to manage the relationship between teens and digital technology. Schools can't do much about young people owning mobile devices, but they *can* issue general guidance to parents about the associated benefits and risks.

Make it clear to parents that screen time *per se* is not the problem. It is what young people are *doing* online that matters. Parents need to think about the 3Cs (context, content and connection): *where* are their children engaging with digital technology, *what* are they doing online and *who* are they connecting with?

- Parents can understandably adopt a 'head in the sand' approach to the content that young people view online. Both in school and at home, it's useful to have discussions that help young people become critical consumers of what they see and digest. This absolutely requires home–school partnership.
- We know that nationally young people's mental health is suffering and that young women are particularly struggling. Schools must make parents aware that they need to keep an eye on the extent to which their child benefits from their digital diet (or not). Parents must be made aware that an over-dependency on 'likes' isn't a healthy or reliable way to measure one's own self-worth.
- It is imperative that both teachers and parents take an active role in emphasising to young people how important digital hygiene is, being discerning and critical about what one is viewing online, and more aware of one's own digital tattoo.

Teaching tip

With universities, colleges and employers increasingly researching potential applications through initial 'Google' checks, the importance of the concept of a 'digital tattoo' cannot be underestimated.

Taking it further

Encourage parents and students to adopt the 'Granny test' when it comes to what they post online. Would granny approve or tut?

Setting the course for coursework

'We can spot the students whose parents provide the support and those that don't.'

When schools set coursework for students, it is often met with a sigh of despair among parents.

We clearly don't want parents doing the work for students, but we can help level the playing field when we set coursework and give instructive guidance to all parents on how best to support their children.

- The information that you give to students about the coursework should not mirror the information that you give parents.
- Parents need to know the purpose of the larger pieces of coursework. Why have you set it? What does it count for? What do you want the young people to get out of it? What's the end game? And when is it due?
- Parents need to know what you are looking for (for example, an essay that is structured with lots of details about the topic).
- Let parents know how to support their child with the project. Is there a list of extra reading books, websites or other sources that they can help their child to access? Is there a local museum to visit with their children?
- Supply parents with a checklist of things to ask their child about over the period they are working on the coursework.
- Parents (and students) appreciate knowing what they are aiming for. Is there an e-version of a coursework submission from previous years that you thought was outstanding? Share it and say why. Perhaps make a short video about what you or examiners are looking for when the work is marked.

Study skills – mind the gap!

'I have no idea how to help him with revision. I just leave him to it.'

Where parents are educated and experienced in taking (and passing) exams, their children may well be more skilled-up in revision.

But millions of students do not have the luxury of parents who already understand how to hone exam and revision skills and memorise large chunks of text. But schools can play a role in levelling the playing field here.

- Invite parents to study skills evenings (way in advance of exam years). Discuss questions like what are examiners looking for in a GCSE English language essay? How do examiners mark GCSE science papers? What are common reasons why students might be marked down? What do we know about memorising? What techniques does the school use to help students?
- Talk to parents about the importance of helping students to be organised. Discuss positive home learning environments and the difference they make to student progress and achievement.
- We worked with a school that sent video tips to the parents of a group of students who were not expected to do particularly well at GCSE. The video resources modelled how to motivate a teen to sit down and study, told parents exactly when the assessments and tests were taking place, and gave them some questions that they could use to initiate a conversation about learning with their children. As an end result, the parents realised that they had an important role to play in preparing children for GCSEs and grew in confidence, while the students felt that their parents cared (perhaps more so than they originally did).

Teaching tip

Reiterate to parents that no question is too simple. Be a school that welcomes questions, warmly invites parental support when it comes to revision and sets the tone for genuine parent–teacher partnership through deeds, not just words.

Taking it further

Nudging rather than pushing matters in homes where parents are supportive of student learning. Try to encourage parents to understand that the little things can boost student learning.

It's OK not to know the answer (helping parents towards mastery)

'It's easy when your kids are little – you know the answers to the questions they ask. Now they're teenagers, I don't even understand the question sometimes!' (Parent)

Many of us understand the transition that the parent above is facing. When children are younger, they tend to ask questions that are fairly easily answered. But as children grow, their questions become more complex and difficult to answer.

Sometimes difficult questions are based around subjects: 'Mum, how does this equation work?' Sometimes they're about life in general: 'Dad, why are there wars?' We suspect that most parents face these issues, and when children get into secondary schools the questions may seem almost impossible to answer.

One important thing you as a teacher can do for parents is to share some of your experiences and the skills you already have. What do you say to a student who approaches you and says 'Miss/Sir, I can't do this!' You almost certainly say something supportive and encouraging, like 'You can – just not yet' or perhaps 'OK, where do you think we should look for the answer?' It's important that we let parents know these simple phrases and skills and, importantly, that it's OK to say 'I don't know'.

- Consider putting something on the website or in a newsletter with the heading 'It's OK not to know!' and the information in this idea.
- Share some stock phrases with parents that you use all the time: 'You don't know how to do it yet', 'Where should we look for the answer?', 'How might you find the answer?'

Parents and homework

'They should be able to do it on their own now. I can't keep up anyhow.' (Parent)

The research literature has some interesting things to say about homework for students in secondary school, and about the role of parents in relation to homework.

There are a number of things that seem **not** to work, in relation to young people's outcomes. These include:

- parents teaching course content
- parents giving young people academic help that they haven't asked for
- parents concentrating on grades or marks rather than on the learning process
- young people feeling that parents are monitoring them very closely and being critical.

It is, of course, possible that these things are related to lower outcomes for students because the parents of struggling students are more likely to be involved in these particular approaches. However, we can't discount the fact that these things simply may not be helpful.

There are, however, some things that **do** seem to work for secondary students. These include:

- what has been called the 'more subtle' aspects of parental engagement, including conversations around learning and general support
- having a 'mastery orientation' – seeing obstacles, failures and setbacks as opportunities rather than as doors that have closed
- concentrating on the learning, rather than on the mark.

> **Bonus idea**
>
> Try pulling the tips from this idea together in a series of podcasts for the school website, or in short, easy-to-read documents on the website. Remember how busy parents are!

Use effective praise with teenagers (and their parents!)

'Effective praise motivates and inspires young people. It makes them want to do something great all over again.'

It is important that both teachers and parents use what is termed 'effective praise' with teenagers.

It is easy to forget to use praise in the context of a busy school day. But when a student is behaving as you wish them to in the classroom or the corridor, then it is important to acknowledge it – as you know. It's the same with parents. As busy as you are, it is important to take a tiny moment out of your day to spot their 'good behaviour' and praise it. In general, praising effectively includes:

- Observe and notice, and make comment on the good things.
- It's important to let parents know that there is value in students' effort rather than just in their success.
- Ask colleagues for phrases that they use when praising students. Collate the list and share it with parents. Perhaps make it accessible on the website.
- Share with the parent community general strategies for motivating students that work for staff.
- Once you have this list, save it along with all the other resources that you are amassing, so that you don't have to create it next year.

Bonus idea ★

Remember to keep track of the positive comments to parents as well as the negative. That way, you can see whether the middle-band young people – who cause no concern – are being neglected!

Who does what?
(Teacher vs parent roles)

'Parents are their first teacher in so many ways, but we are the experts in school-based learning. Both roles need to be respected.' (Teacher)

There is an ongoing discourse in some places about making school 'more like home' and, occasionally, making home more like school.

We're not convinced either is a good idea; schools and homes don't have the same functions, and making either over in the guise of the other is neither useful nor helpful for students. The spheres *overlap*, in that learning obviously goes on in both places, but the two need to remain separate, if connected.

The roles of teacher and parent can overlap because:

- You both care about the young person.
- You both want the best for that young person.
- You both want the young person to learn, grow and develop.

But the roles also differ:

- For the parent, that young person is one of the most important people in the world. For the teacher, while the young person is important, they are one among many.
- The teacher has a professional relationship with the young person, however warm and well-meaning that relationship may be. The parent has a personal and familial relationship with the young person.
- The teacher is primarily interested in the learning of the young person, and all other areas that impact on learning are seen in that light. The parent is primarily interested in the young person as a whole.

Teaching tip

Remember it's not your job as a teacher to parent the majority of young people who pass through your classroom. We are not making suggestions about where the lines should be drawn, as these lines can be slightly different for each individual student.

Teaching tip

Parents tend to want to know that you *like* their child and value their mental health and wellbeing, and then they will be amenable to discussing their progress at school and how they can help.

The parents you never see

'We never see them. They never come in, no matter what we do. What are we doing wrong?'

If you've ever encountered either of the authors in an official capacity, the chances are that you've been asked to jettison the phrase 'hard-to-reach parents'. Yet we know that the phrase — and the idea — is alive and well in many schools.

Teaching tip

As we've said throughout this book, it's about creating relationships. In the case of some parents, you may be trying to build relationships on the jagged ruins that others have left behind, meaning that you (as a teacher) are trying to build a relationship with someone who has had bad experiences with teachers before.

The phrase 'hard to reach' denotes the parents who 'never come in', don't answer the phone, don't pick up emails and don't respond to texts. These things are demonstrable facts. The problem arises when these facts are extrapolated beyond what might be called their legitimate cognitive load. For example: 'We never see Mrs Jones — she just doesn't care about her kids.' The fact that you don't see her is simply reporting what does (not) happen, but the second part of the sentence isn't fair.

Think about it this way — if a young person is struggling in your subject, is your first thought that they just don't care? That could be the case, or it could be that they really are struggling with the subject matter, no matter how much they care. Good teachers learn the difference.

We know that the vast majority of parents love their children (including their teenagers) and want the best for them. We also know that parents often find teachers frightening, school grounds daunting and coming to school an anxiety-inducing process, to the extent that some parents just avoid it altogether. This does **not** mean that they don't love their children or that they don't care about their education, schooling or learning. It may mean, however, that you have to go the extra mile (often, literally, by moving out of school) to connect with these parents.

Reflect then innovate

'By sharing important dates with parents and giving them ideas of how they could help, students felt better supported.' (Headteacher)

A headteacher of a large secondary school once contacted one of the authors and asked whether we could help engage a particular cohort of parents who were seemingly uninterested in their child's progress, particularly their upcoming GCSE exams.

We set out to create a support system for the parents, alongside that for the students. It was an experiment; we wanted to prove that by empowering the parent, the student might be more motivated to work harder over some critical months. We don't have the space here to describe the whole project, but the important thing is that it worked. What did we do?

- We made sure that parents were aware that their children had huge academic potential but were acting like 'Ferraris in a garage'; their potential was not being realised.
- We named it the 'Learning Boost Project' so parents knew we were taking it seriously.
- We made parents aware of resources we had created to help them support their child with revision. Short video clips were emailed out each week, with suggestions of how parents might encourage their children.
- Simply making sure that parents knew about key assessments made a difference. They could remind students but also, importantly, show that these things mattered to them. Parents were showing students that they cared.
- A mentoring programme was set up for the students, and parents were invited in for chats about progress.
- The students' GCSE results ended up much more positive than had been originally predicted. Importantly, parents realised that they had a role to play in supporting learning.

Teaching tip

Simply texting parents that tests are coming up has been shown to be effective in improving achievement, but the process outlined in this idea is likely to have a much more lasting effect!

Keep talking

'If parents aren't the source of everything, the internet will be.'
(A professor of adolescent and child mental health)

Any parent of a teen knows that as soon as they hit the edge of adolescence, things change. In the place of an obedient, compliant child comes a teen who enjoys challenging your authority, ideas and suggestions.

Parents have to evolve to be able to maintain the positive relationship they enjoyed with their child previously. One of the most important things you can do for parents is to simply let them know that they are not alone and they are not the only parent who has struggled (or is struggling) with the younger but not-so-young-anymore members of their families. Suggest the following approaches:

- Allow the teenager more freedom to contest ideas, debate and develop their voice. Show parents that as a school you value teens' ability to debate, and teens often have some wonderful, innovative and disruptive ideas! We need to value this.
- Suggest that parents don't insist upon face-to-face formal chats and instead try the 'side by side' chats that accompany doing a task together. Parents of teens often complain that communication is nearly impossible. You spend all day with teenagers; what works for you?
- Show teenagers that you respect their viewpoint and value it too.
- Encourage parents to partake in as much 'family talk' as possible, debating, discussing and chewing the fat about a range of social and political issues. You might want to give them some conversational prompts that will help them get going!

'Proud of you' letters

'You've no idea how proud your parents were of you.' (Relative)

We were recently talking about the phrase above and we all agreed that we really did have no idea how proud our parents were, because they'd never told us. We only found out from friends and family after our parents were no longer able to tell us...

Often, we find it difficult to say 'I'm proud of you' to our children. We may fear that it will make them 'big-headed' or arrogant; we may fear that if we praise them and point out their efforts, they will stop trying hard. We may feel that they need us, as parents (or teachers), to constantly show them how to improve.

One of the schools we worked with in a recent project tried to find a way around this, and suggested to parents of incoming Year 7 students that they write to their children and tell them 'Why I'm proud of you'. The school found that parents often seemed more able to write these things down than say them.

- If you decide to do this, be sure to give parents enough guidance, perhaps producing a template or sample letter.
- Think carefully about *all* the young people involved – do all of them have someone who will write the letter? If not, can you or someone else write the letter?
- Consider whether it's better to ask adults to write this letter or have the young people think what they themselves are proud of?
- The timing of asking parents to partake in this exercise matters; again, at the point of transition or that first term back, we want students to hit the ground running, knowing that their parents value education and are proud of them, but also have expectations for how they apply themselves to their schoolwork.

Teaching tip

Once you've produced the sample letter, make sure that you keep a copy of it, indexed, so that the next person who wants to use it can find it!

Parent peer support

'We never see the other parents, so we never get the sort of information we used to get at the school gate.'

One of the many changes that happen when children move up to secondary school is that parents often (and often suddenly) lack a daily interaction with other parents and carers.

Where once parents would have met one another at the school gate, young people in secondary school often make their way to and from school on their own. Parents have told us that they often feel adrift, and that the move to secondary school has been like 'having the security blanket pulled away from you'. Yet we also know that parent-to-parent support can be a vital lifeline and support; research tells us this but so does simple experience. As parents, many of us have known the relief of having another parent say something as simple as 'Oh, yes, mine does that' or 'Mine used to do that – here's how we got over it'.

Luckily, there are still lots of places where parents can mingle and meet each other:

- parents' evenings or consultation days
- open days
- sports days
- concerts
- fairs
- PTA and other parent-facing meetings.

Parent-to-parent work is more useful – and more likely to work and be sustained – if it's initiated and supported by parents. It may require staff to suggest things, but this may be a classic case of lighting a blue touch paper and standing back. However, it may be that a little bit of ingenuity is needed on your part to start some of the fruitful conversations that can arise at these events.

Sustainable practice

Part 8

It's everyone's job

'I don't have time to work with parents; that's what the pastoral staff and head of year are for!'

The trouble with having specific parental engagement (PE) officers in schools, or family liaison workers, is that the rest of the staff may feel that everything to do with working with families can be left at their door.

Teaching tip

Whatever you do, remember to evaluate it! Any new initiative requires ideal outcomes, a plan of action and a way of evaluating whether or not it has been successful.

What is optimal is that all staff work hard to support parental engagement and strong partnerships with the local community. When everyone is doing their job, the burden on the family worker or PE officer is reduced, which is necessary so that she or he can truly get on the job of supporting those most in need.

If you do have an assigned family support worker or PE officer, make sure that you understand exactly what their role is (we have discovered that in some schools, PE officers are providing food and basics to the most disadvantaged families and are completely inundated with the demand for their time). In an ideal world, PE officers would be able to focus on learning and working in unison with colleagues to ensure all families feel supported enough to support their children in turn.

PE officers (where the focus is on learning) can support colleagues by:

- doing biannual audits of how parents are feeling in terms of being able to support their children
- running focus groups with parents across year groups, where they are able to explore more about the parent–school partnership and where the gaps are
- understanding more about the challenges that students face at home and how, as a school, such stresses can be alleviated.

Have a party!

'We aren't very good, on the whole, at celebrating what we do well. We are so focused on the students that we forget to give ourselves a pat on the back.'

It is important that home–school partnerships are so highly valued in your setting that when success is apparent (students thriving directly as a result of it), it is a cause of celebration, discussion and reflection among staff.

When we advocate celebrating what is going – and what has gone – well in the home–school partnership, we don't expect you to set aside resources or ring-fence money for a party of the balloon-and-cake kind. Examples from our experience include:

- parent and staff surveys that have resulted in an identified area of concern and then, together, doing something about it
- a PTA, together with staff, engaging in fundraising activities to boost the content of the school library
- parent champions being photographed with teachers on transition evenings as a 'team' who have contributed to the success of the evening
- current parents and staff making a 'Welcome to our school' video and collaborating in a way that is impactful and also fun
- celebrating the academic success of students where parents were supported by staff to help with their revision.

In short, parents and teachers need to be seen innovating and working together with the objective of helping young people to thrive. You know that you already support students and their families on an individual basis, but sometimes, your hard work and theirs need to be visible. Why not inspire the school community with the story?

Teaching tip

Just as we encourage students to adopt a growth mindset and to be unafraid to try new things out, we need to adopt the same approach to exploring strategies for engaging parents. Whatever you want to try to achieve, be honest with parents. Some things will work, some won't, but at least we are trying!

Not my circus, not my monkeys

'This simian belongeth not to me.'

The phrase 'not my circus, not my monkeys' is an English translation of a Polish phrase and it means what it says on the tin: this isn't my problem.

This idea, in essence, is giving you permission to say 'no'. We don't think anyone would try to put everything in this book into practice, but just in case that's crossed your mind: please don't! Just as you can't put into effect every good idea about teaching that crosses your path (or Twitter feed), you can't put into effect every idea in this book. And it wouldn't be appropriate even to try!

Not all the ideas will be right for your school or your families. Some ideas need to build on previous work. Relationships take time to develop and consolidate.

- Avoid what's been called 'Civil Service-itis', which goes like this: 'Something must be done. This is something. Therefore, we will do it.'
- Instead, take the time to work through what will be best for *your* school and *your* families – that takes time.
- Parental engagement is one area where parents won't be holding you to account. It isn't necessarily expected that secondary schools reach out to parents to develop constructive partnerships. Set your school apart by saying that you value and want to invest in that partnership. Be trailblazers. Amaze the parents with your passion for building a partnership that has at its centre one concern: optimal ways for students to thrive.

Every failure is an opportunity

'Failing is hard but it is what we learn from it that matters. We try to instil that in our students.' (Teacher)

You no doubt tell your students that failure, rather than understanding, is the first step to success. The same is true of your work with parents.

Will everything in this book work perfectly – for your parents, for your families – the first time you try it, right out of the gate? As much as we believe in what we've written here, the answer is almost certainly 'no', and for reasons that we've already highlighted a number of times: each cohort of parents is different, just as every year group of students is different.

- Don't give up on an activity because it was not well attended – you need to give up on the activities that don't have an effect. The two are not necessarily the same thing. If something worked for one or two parents, that may be the launch pad that you need to make things work more widely. Ask what worked, highlight it and go from there.
- Some of the ideas in this book require you to have a good relationship with your parents – but that doesn't happen overnight and it doesn't happen quickly, particularly for parents who have jaundiced views of school because of their own experiences.
- You therefore need to think carefully about not only *what* to do but *when* to do it – and not just when in the year, but when in your relationship with parents.

Don't start from scratch

'It is exciting when you realise you don't need to start from scratch. We have already set the wheel in motion in many cases.'

One of the reasons why we've suggested keeping records of your work with parents is precisely so that you *don't* have to start from scratch.

Teaching tip

You're also standing on the shoulders of giants. Look around for resources to support your work with parents. Look online (and don't neglect collection sites, such as Pinterest) and talk to colleagues in other schools.

Keeping detailed records will give you a bank or body of ideas to go back to and work from. Of course, that's not really a lot of help if you are at the very beginning of this journey – you need to build up those ideas before they can be used.

That doesn't mean, however, that you really are starting from scratch.

- If you've been in teaching for a while, you almost certainly have some good experiences of your own in relation to working with parents. Don't neglect those – write them down, record them and think about them.
- If you're very new to teaching, you quite possibly have a formal (or even informal) mentor. Ask them about their work with parents – what have they done in the past that worked well? And if they are willing to share what hasn't worked as well, discuss why it didn't work.

Being a reflective practitioner

'I never get time to think in this job!' (Every teacher we speak to!)

We know how busy teachers are and how difficult it can be to find the time to be reflective – to do all those things that they told you about in your teacher training, like keeping a research journal and keeping track of what you read (and what you want to read) and all the ideas you have that will be perfect for next year...

It's the same with work with parents; all through this book, we've been asking you not just to *do* but to *think about doing* – to think about what you might want to change and how those changes could come into being.

- Thinking – deep, reflective thinking – doesn't happen by chance.
- Thinking also doesn't happen without time.

We therefore have some suggestions about reflecting on practice in working with parents (but of course, a lot of these ideas would apply to other areas as well!).

- Take time in staff or departmental meetings to have 'thinking time' – and actually give time to thinking. Have five minutes in every staff meeting to just 'think about X' – obviously, we want you to start with thinking about parents!
- We also know how much can get lost in the busy lives of teachers and schools – hence our ideas about keeping track of things. Have a board in the staff room or department room where people can post 'good ideas' about working with parents.
- It's worth noting, as well, that failures really are chances to grow (just like you tell students!). Keep track of what didn't work as well as what did – not just the fact that it didn't work but also *why* it didn't work.

Teaching tip

A lot of the ideas in this book – such as the ones around barriers and languages – would lend themselves to being part of the 'thinking time' in staff meetings or departmental meetings.

Utilise the expertise already around

'Everybody knows she's the one who really gets on with the parents.'

There is always someone in school who is better at talking to parents than other colleagues. Perhaps they even enjoy it!

These people may be best placed to train other staff on what works in terms of phoning home, writing letters to parents and those difficult chats with parents that teachers can dread. We are *all* learners – students, parents and teachers. Teachers spend a great deal of time updating their skills and gaining new ones – this area is no different. Remember to look for expertise beyond the teachers; a TA may have more experience or expertise in working with parents than most teachers.

- If your school has a parental engagement officer or worker, ask them for their advice or to present at an INSET day. It is important in this case to show that SLT support the work that is being done and the training given.
- If your school doesn't have anyone in these roles, look around to neighbouring schools – do they have staff who would be willing to come in and support your school?
- Don't think just about secondary staff – sometimes those with the most experience of working directly with parents are in primary or Early Years. This could be an interesting collaboration; work with a colleague from these phases, particularly from a feeder school, to see what practices could be adapted to your school.
- Make sure that ideas and even materials (taking care not to infringe copyright!) from any training attended by staff members are shared with everyone as far as possible.

Bonus idea ★

It can be liberating for less experienced colleagues to hear from colleagues who have years of experience with parents and to know that they, too, once dreaded conversations with parents but have honed their skills down to a fine art. Experienced staff will have quick tips, tweaks and ideas for those trickier chats with parents – make sure you create the space for this exchange of ideas to take place!

Using the skills you have

'I don't have time to learn anything new!' (Almost every teacher when asked to take on a new scheme of work or area of expertise)

We understand how time-poor most teachers are, and that the idea of taking on a new initiative is daunting, to say the least.

We also know the likely reaction in most staff rooms to any suggestion of new practices or anything that adds to workload in any way – for good reason, teachers are wary of new things that will take time and possibly not show good results.

- Many of the ideas that we're suggesting in this book are not actually new – they are consolidations of things that probably already go on but no one has collated before.
- Some of the suggestions that we make will take time at the outset. But they will eventually save you a lot of time in the long run – it's better to expend a little bit of time now to save hours down the line.
- Some of the things that we're suggesting are more of a shift than a new thing – often, we're asking you to use skills that you already have, and indeed use daily, in a new way:
  - We're asking you to use your skills in planning in relation to events for parents.
  - We're asking you to use your skills in data capture to evaluate the work you do with parents.
  - You are very skilled in helping people to learn new things and supporting learning; we're asking you not only to use those skills appropriately with parents (to help them learn how to support learning), but also to share those skills with parents.

Taking it further

Use time in a staff meeting or INSET day to ask everyone to list the skills they think are needed in working to support parental engagement. Collate these, and bring them back to another meeting, as a 'list of skills' (without saying what the skills relate to). Ask people to tick the ones they have and then reveal that these are skills for supporting parents, and take the conversation from there.

Not quite finis...

'You only grow by coming to the end of something and by beginning.'

This isn't the last idea. It may be the last idea that WE have, but the whole point of this book – and others like it – is that the book is just a starting point, a stepping-off point.

Teachers are remarkably good at 'pick up and reuse' and 'make do and mend'. We've already given you lots of ideas here (99 of them!), but these need to be adapted, changed and reworked so that they fit your individual school and the families that you work with.

Like it or not, they will also need *constant* adaptation – you don't teach exactly the same lesson every year, even if you cover the same topics; you adjust, you change and you might use different examples, because you have different students.

As we've previously pointed out, parents are just young people who grew up – and so they are different, one from the other, just as your students are. One year group of parents will not be the same as the next, just as one year group of students is not the same.

- Use the ideas in this book as a starting point.
- You don't have to do everything – you can't do everything! Choose the tips and ideas that are best for *your* school and for *your* families.
- Keep records.
- Share! You aren't in this alone – it really does take a village (or a city or a town) to raise a child, and it takes the same to educate young people.